MW01016303

The Power™ Of: 1-2-3™

by

Robert E. Williams

A SPECTRUM BOOK

Management Information Source, Inc.

Copyright 1983 by Management Information Source, Inc.
3543 N.E. Broadway, Portland, Oregon 97232
(503) 287-1462

Second Printing

ISBN 0-13-687525-4

All rights reserved. Reproduction or use, without express permission, of editorial or pictorial content, in any manner, is prohibited. No patent liability is assumed with respect to the use of the information contained herein. While every precaution has been taken in the preparation of this book, the publisher assumes no responsibility for errors or omissions. Neither is any liability assumed for damages resulting from the use of the information contained herein.

1-2-3 is a trademark of Lotus Development Corporation
Cambridge, Mass.
(617) 492-7171

The Power Of: is a trademark of Management Information Source, Inc.

Edited by: Estelle Phillips

ONE OF A SERIES OF INSTRUCTION MANUALS ON THE USE AND
APPLICATION OF COMPUTER PROGRAMS

PREFACE

The Power Of: 1-2-3 is a book of exercises designed especially for users and potential users of the 1-2-3 computer program. By performing these simple step-by-step exercises, you will rapidly gain an ability to utilize the broad range of 1-2-3 capabilities that make it a most powerful software program available for personal size computers.

Better than an instruction book, The Power Of: 1-2-3 demonstrates the use of 1-2-3 features through specific application samples.

The Power Of: 1-2-3 will show you how to apply the many functions of 1-2-3, such as its built-in Data Base, Keyboard Macros, Graphing, and many other powerful functions and commands, no matter what your applications. These ten easy-to-follow exercises are designed to help you understand and use 1-2-3 operations. Business owners, accountants, financial analysts, stock brokers, homeowners, manufacturers, engineers, educators, scientists, architects, students, or anyone with a problem that can be solved using a computer, will find The Power Of: 1-2-3 an invaluable companion to their 1-2-3 program.

No special training is needed to benefit from the exercises in The Power Of: 1-2-3. All instructions are in plain English. The logic of each step is clearly spelled out, so you can later apply the information to your specific needs. The Power Of: 1-2-3 will become your most valuable reference book as you expand your use of 1-2-3.

IF YOU OWN, OR ARE THINKING OF OWNING, 1-2-3, YOU SHOULD OWN THIS BOOK!

INTRODUCTION

The exercises in this book have been purposely designed to provide an opportunity to easily follow the logic of 1-2-3 functions, and then apply those functions to specific problems. It is important to note that the problems in the exercises have been specifically selected to demonstrate 1-2-3, as opposed to illustrating specific problem-solving methods.

Each exercise in The Power Of: 1-2-3 is self-contained. Each demonstrates some special ability or abilities that will broaden your knowledge and skills in using 1-2-3 as a problem-solving tool for your special applications.

The 1-2-3 format is arranged on the computer screen in columns and rows. The 1-2-3 worksheet format is illustrated in Figure 1 with a grid superimposed on it to offer a visual concept for the following explanation.

The 1-2-3 worksheet columns are identified by letter designations, the rows by numbers. Each position where a column and row intersect is a "coordinate" location. Visualizing your worksheet as a street map, you can locate any coordinate on your worksheet using a letter and a number designation (such as B4) to identify its distinctive column and row intersection.

The relationships between values in coordinates on your worksheet are determined by simple instructions entered into the coordinates in the form of algebraic formulas. (Don't get panicky; that just means (a + b) and other similar expressions.) By visualizing the street map grid image and following the exercises, you will easily and quickly catch on to the power of 1-2-3 and how it can work for you.

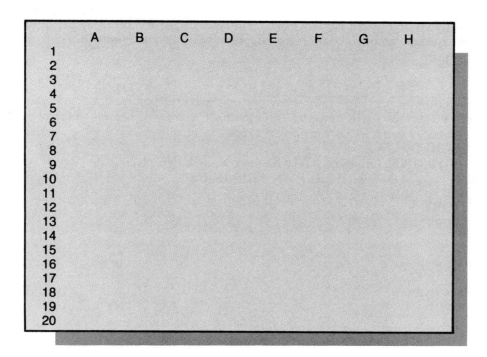

Figure 1

CONTENTS

EXERCISE ONE

MAINTAINING A STOCK PORTFOLIO

DESCRIPTION

The Lotus 1-2-3 program has many built-in commands and functions, two of the more powerful ones will be demonstrated in this exercise: Data Base and Graphics.

To demonstrate these capabilities, we have set up a stock portfolio exercise where we will maintain the stock portfolio with current and past information on stocks and then draw out information from the worksheet using different criteria, for example: stocks with a gain; changing the criteria to display stocks with a loss; and then simultaneously graphing this information.

OPERATIONS PERFORMED

Setting Up The Worksheet Format

Entering Mathematical Formulas

Setting Up a Data Base

Graphing the Data

Viewing the Graph

Saving

Printing the Worksheet

Printing the Graph

Making New Entries into the Data Criteria

FUNCTIONS USED

AVG
SUM

COMMANDS USED

COPY	copies formulas
DATA	defines Input range
	defines Output range
	defines Criteria range
	executes Query of data base
GRAPHIC	
FILE	saves worksheet
FILE	retrieves (loads)
PRINT	prints worksheet
RANGE	erases
RANGE	centers labels
RANGE	formats in percent
REPEAT	repeats dashed lines
SAVE	saves graph
WORKSHEET	deletes row

SETTING UP THE WORKSHEET FORMAT

Using the following directions, set up your worksheet by copying Figure 1 exactly as it is illustrated, retaining exact row and column locations of all information.

	A	B	C	D	E	F	G	H	I	J	K	L	M	N
1	Risk Free Return		0.12											
2	------------------													
3	Company			Purchase	Market	Purchase	Market				Expected	Return		
4	Name	Ticker	Shares	PPrice	MPrice	PGross	MGross	Gain $	Gain %	Beta	Return	Ratio	Low Est	High Est
5	---
6	
7	
8	
9	
10	
11	
12	
13	
14	===
15	Sub Totals
16	Cash On Hand
17	===
18	Totals

Figure 1

Enter your column headings.

After entering your column headings, you will center them in the columns by using the Center option.

Place your cursor on A3 and type:

/R	starts RANGE command
L	selects Label-Prefix option
C	selects Center option and displays Range of labels A3..A3

Move your cursor to N4. Notice the screen is reversing to show you what coordinates are to be formatted.

RETURN	executes the command

To enter dashed lines on your worksheet, place your cursor on the left-most column of the row where you want the line (A5 in this example.)

Type:

\	starts REPEAT command
—	label to be repeated
RETURN	executes the command

The column your cursor is on will now have a line of dashes across its width. To extend the dashed line in the same row across the remaining columns, leave your cursor where it is and type:

/C	starts COPY command and displays Range to copy from
RETURN	displays Range to copy to
B5	first coordinate to copy to
.	ellipsis—indicates from-to
N5	last coordinate to copy to
RETURN	executes the command

The dashed line will now appear extended across the columns you have indicated by your coordinates. To enter a double-dashed line on the worksheet, repeat the operations above, using the symbol = as your label to be repeated.

ENTERING MATHEMATICAL FORMULAS

You will now begin entering mathematical formulas that will establish the relationships between column and row positions. The formulas and their locations are illustrated in Figure 2.

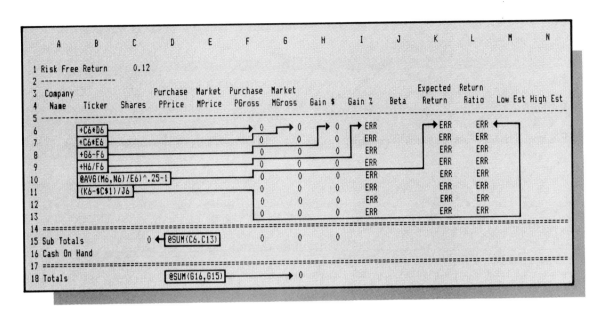

Figure 2

Formula one, in the Purchase Gross column, multiplies the Shares times the Purchase Price.

Place your cursor on F6 and type:

+	prepares the coordinate to accept a numeric expression
C6	coordinate containing Shares
*	multiplies
D6	coordinate containing Purchase Price
RETURN	enters the formula

Formula two, in the Market Gross column, multiplies the Shares times the Market Price.

Place your cursor on G6 and type:

+	prepares the coordinate to accept a numeric expression

C6	coordinate containing Shares
*	multiplies
E6	coordinate containing Market Price
RETURN	enters the formula

Formula three, in the Gain $ column, subtracts Purchase Gross from Market Gross.

Place your cursor on H6 and type:

+	prepares the coordinate to accept a numeric expression
G6	coordinate containing Market Gross
—	subtracts
F6	coordinate containing Purchase Gross
RETURN	enters the formula

Formula four, in the Gain % column, gives you the percent of dollars gained, by dividing Gain $ by Purchase Gross.

Place your cursor on I6 and type:

+	prepares the coordinate to accept a numeric expression
H6	coordinate containing Gain $
/	divides
F6	coordinate containing Purchase Gross
RETURN	enters the formula

To display the value as a percent, 1-2-3 allows you to format the coordinate to show a percent sign and automatically moves the decimal place to two places to the right.

To do this, leave your cursor on I6 and type:

/R	starts RANGE command
F	selects Format option
P	selects Percent option
2	number of decimal places

RETURN	displays range to format
RETURN	executes the command

An ERR will be displayed until values are entered in the appropriate columns because of the division by zero.

Formula five, in the Expected Return column, first generates the average of the High and Low Estimates, then divides that by the Market Price. Then the result is taken to the .25 power and 1 is subtracted from it, which gives you the percentage per year of a four-year period.

The High and the Low Estimates, in this exercise, were taken from the Value Line Investment Survey newsletter, which gives you the high and low for a four-year period.

Place your cursor on K6 and type:

(	parenthesis—opens expression
@AVG(	averages the following list
M6	coordinate containing Low Est
,	comma—separates values in list
N6)	coordinate containing High Est
/	divides
E6	coordinate containing Market Price
)	parenthesis—closes expression
^.25	takes the value generated to the .25 power
—1	subtracts 1
RETURN	enters the formula

Formula six, in the Return Ratio column, subtracts the Risk Free Return from the Expected Return percentage, which is then divided by the Beta percentage.

The Beta percentage was taken from the Value Line Investment Survey newsletter.

──────────────────── **NOTE** ────────────────────

1-2-3 is designed to do one of two things with coordinates when they are copied. The coordinates are either relative to their new location or they remain absolute, which means they remain the same.

A coordinate address is relative unless it is converted to an absolute by having a dollar sign ($) preceding the column designation and/or row designation, i.e., ($G$8).

A quick way to make a coordinate absolute is by putting the cursor on that coordinate and pressing the F4 key, which will place the dollar as shown automatically.

Place your cursor on L6 and type:

(K6	coordinate containing Expected Return
—	subtracts
$C$1)	coordinate containing Risk Free Return Note: The dollar signs turn the coordinate into an absolute address.
/	divides
J6	coordinate containing Beta
RETURN	enters the value

To display Expected Return and Return Ratio as percentages, leave your cursor on any location and type:

/R	starts RANGE command
F	selects Format option
P	selects Percent option
2	number of decimal places
RETURN	displays range to format
K6.L6	range
RETURN	executes the command

The next operation is to copy the formulas just entered down their appropriate columns, between the single and double dash lines.

Leave your cursor on any location and type:

/C	starts COPY command and displays Range to copy from
F6	first coordinate to copy from
•	ellipsis—indicates from-to

L6	last coordinate to copy from
RETURN	displays range to copy to
F7	first coordinate to copy to
.	ellipsis—indicates from-to
F13	last coordinate to copy to
RETURN	executes the command

Formula seven, in the Sub Total row in the Shares column, adds the total shares.

Place your cursor on C15 and type:

@SUM(	adds values in following list
C6	first coordinate in list
.	ellipsis—indicates from-to
C13)	last coordinate in list
RETURN	enters the formula

Copy formula seven across the row into the Purchase Gross, Market Gross and Gain $ columns.

Leave your cursor on C15 and type:

/C	starts COPY command and displays range to copy from
RETURN	displays range to copy to
F15	first coordinate to copy to
.	ellipsis—indicates from-to
H15	last coordinate to copy to
RETURN	executes the command

Formula eight, in the Totals row, Market Gross column, adds the Market Gross subtotal to Cash On Hand.

Place your cursor on G18 and type:

@SUM(	adds values in the list
G16	coordinate containing Cash On Hand
,	comma—separates values in list

G15)   coordinate containing Market Gross
                                      subtotal

RETURN   enters the formula

Now that the formulas are entered, enter the values as illustrated in Figure 3. Enter into the following columns: Ticker, Shares, PPrice, MPrice, Beta, Low Est and High Est. Enter the Cash on Hand amount. Do not make entries into columns which contain formulas, or the formulas will be erased.

	A	B	C	D	E	F	G	H	I	J	K	L	M	N
1	Risk Free Return		0.12											
2	----------													
3	Company			Purchase	Market	Purchase	Market				Expected	Return		
4	Name	Ticker	Shares	PPrice	MPrice	PGross	MGross	Gain $	Gain %	Beta	Return	Ratio	Low Est	High Est
5	----------													
6		bll	300	21	26.25	6300	7875	1575	25.00%	0.8	37.01%	31.26%	85	100
7		cty	325	42	30	13650	9750	-3900	-28.57%	0.9	13.62%	1.80%	40	60
8		dtr	450	17	34	7650	15300	7650	100.00%	0.5	-7.87%	-39.73%	17	32
9		sdt	400	30	34	12000	13600	1600	13.33%	0.9	41.55%	32.83%	127	146
10		ibm	600	56	25	33600	15000	-18600	-55.36%	0.7	34.78%	32.54%	68	97
11		vbn	450	78	25	35100	11250	-23850	-67.95%	0.5	5.10%	-13.81%	29	32
12		lnd	200	60	17	12000	3400	-8600	-71.67%	0.6	59.85%	79.75%	72	150
13		abu	475	75	82	35625	38950	3325	9.33%	0.8	-20.96%	-41.20%	28	36
14	=========													
15	Sub Totals		3200			155925	115125	-40800						
16	Cash On Hand						12000							
17	=========													
18	Totals						127125							

Figure 3

SETTING UP A DATA BASE

1-2-3 has some powerful, built-in commands: a Data and a Graphic command. The data command allows you to define the information into a data base, and the graphic command allows you to plot information instantaneously.

To demonstrate the use of the Data command on the information you have just entered in Figure 3, setting up of the Data base requires three processes: the input, the output and the criteria of the data base. Use the following directions and refer to Figure 4.

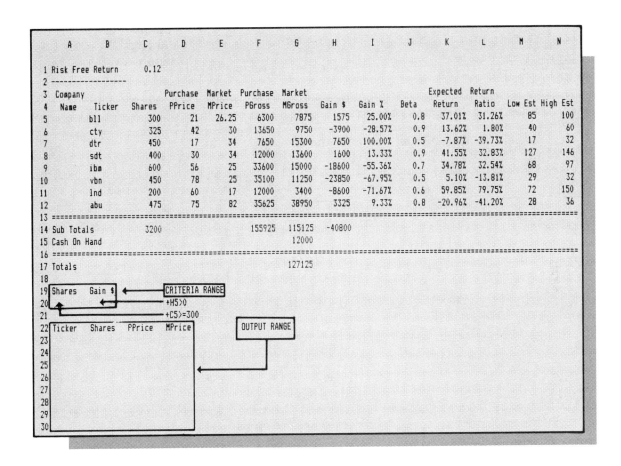

Figure 4

Before defining the input range, you will need to delete Row 5 because your input range, first row, contains title information and the following rows must contain only data information.

To delete Row 5, place your cursor on A5 and type:

/W	starts WORKSHEET command
D	selects Delete option
R	selects Row option
RETURN	executes the command

Then enter Criteria labels and Output labels, which define which columns of information you wish pulled out of the data base.

First you will define the Input range for the data base.

Place your cursor on A4 and type:

/D	starts DATA command
Q	selects Query option
I	selects Input option and displays Input Range
A4	upper left-hand corner of the data base
.	ellipsis—indicates from-to
L12	lower right-hand corner of the data base
RETURN	executes the option

The next operation is to define the Output range for the data base.

O	selects Output option and displays Output Range
A22	upper left-hand corner of the output range
.	ellipsis—indicates from-to
D30	lower right-hand corner of the output range
RETURN	executes the command

The last operation is to define the Criteria range for selecting information out of the database.

C	selects Criteria option and displays Criteria range

A19	upper left-hand corner of Criteria range
.	ellipsis—indicates from-to
B20	lower right-hand corner of Criteria range
RETURN	executes the option
Q	Quits DATA command

To demonstrate the use of this data base, we will enter two formulas in the Criteria range. The first formula in the Shares column will ask to display all stocks with 300 or more shares. The second formula in the Gain $ column will ask for all stocks that have had a gain greater than zero.

We are asking our data base to display, in the Output range, all stocks that have 300 or more shares and have had a gain greater than zero.

Formula Nine in the Criteria range Shares column will select all stocks that have 300 or more shares.

Place your cursor on A20 and type:

+	prepares the coordinate to accept a numeric expression
C5	coordinate containing first data in the Shares column
> =	greater than or equal to
300	value to compare against
RETURN	enters the formula

Formula ten, in the Criteria range Gain $ column, selects all stocks with a gain greater than zero.

Place your cursor on B20 and type:

+	prepares the coordinate to accept a numeric expression
H5	coordinate containing first data in the Gain $ column
>	greater than

0	value to compare against
RETURN	enters the formula

All you need to do to execute the Query of the data base is to type:

/D	starts DATA command
Q	selects Query option
E	selects Extract option
Q	selects Quit option

The data will be selected from the data base and displayed in the Output range as the Criteria called for it, as illustrated in Figure 5.

	A	B	C	D	E	F	G	H	I	J	K	L	M	N
1	Risk Free Return		0.12											
2	-----------------													
3	Company			Purchase	Market	Purchase	Market				Expected	Return		
4	Name	Ticker	Shares	PPrice	MPrice	PGross	MGross	Gain $	Gain %	Beta	Return	Ratio	Low Est	High Est
5		bll	300	21	26.25	6300	7875	1575	25.00%	0.8	37.01%	31.26%	85	100
6		cty	325	42	30	13650	9750	-3900	-28.57%	0.9	13.62%	1.80%	40	60
7		dtr	450	17	34	7650	15300	7650	100.00%	0.5	-7.87%	-39.73%	17	32
8		sdt	400	30	34	12000	13600	1600	13.33%	0.9	41.55%	32.83%	127	146
9		ibm	600	56	25	33600	15000	-18600	-55.36%	0.7	34.78%	32.54%	68	97
10		vbn	450	78	25	35100	11250	-23850	-67.95%	0.5	5.10%	-13.81%	29	32
11		lnd	200	60	17	12000	3400	-8600	-71.67%	0.6	59.85%	79.75%	72	150
12		abu	475	75	82	35625	38950	3325	9.33%	0.8	-20.96%	-41.20%	28	36
13	===													
14	Sub Totals		3200			155925	115125	-40800						
15	Cash On Hand						12000							
16	===													
17	Totals						127125							
18														
19	Shares	Gain $		←	CRITERIA RANGE									
20	1	1												
21														
22	Ticker	Shares	PPrice	MPrice	←	OUTPUT RANGE								
23	bll	300	21	26.25										
24	dtr	450	17	34										
25	sdt	400	30	34										
26	abu	475	75	82										
27														
28														
29														
30														

Figure 5

GRAPHING THE DATA

Now to demonstrate how easy it is to do graphs on the data on your worksheet, we will graph some of the information in the Output range.

Place your cursor on A23 and type:

/G	starts GRAPHIC command
T	selects Type option
B	selects Bar option
X	displays X-axis range
A23	upper left-hand corner of range
•	ellipsis—indicates from-to
A30	lower right-hand corner of range
RETURN	executes the command
A	displays first data range for the Y-axis
C23	upper left-hand corner of range
•	ellipsis—indicates from-to
C30	lower right-hand corner of range
RETURN	executes the command
B	displays second data range for the Y-axis
D23	upper left-hand corner of range
•	ellipsis—indicates from-to
D30	lower right-hand corner of range
RETURN	executes the command

VIEWING THE GRAPH

To view your graph, type:

V	selects View option

Now that you have viewed the graph on your CRT screen, you will want to save it so you can print it out on your printer if your printer has graphic capabilities. Our graphs have been printed on an Epson 100 with graphics package. Refer to Figure 6.

Before saving the graph be sure you have a data disk in your Drive two to save the graph to.

S	selects SAVE option
Ticker	graph file name
RETURN	executes the command
Q	Quits, exits from GRAPH command

Before exiting the main program to the graphics program you will first want to save your worksheet.

SAVING

You may wish to save your entire worksheet. To do this leave your cursor on any location and type:

/F	starts FILE command
S	selects SAVE option

Type in name of file. Do not leave spaces between words.

RETURN	executes the command

PRINTING

To print out all or a portion of your worksheet, use the following directions, which are given for the Epson printer (compressed font).

Place your cursor on A1 and type:

/P	starts PRINT command
P	displays options
O	selects Options option
S	selects Setup option and displays Enter Setup String

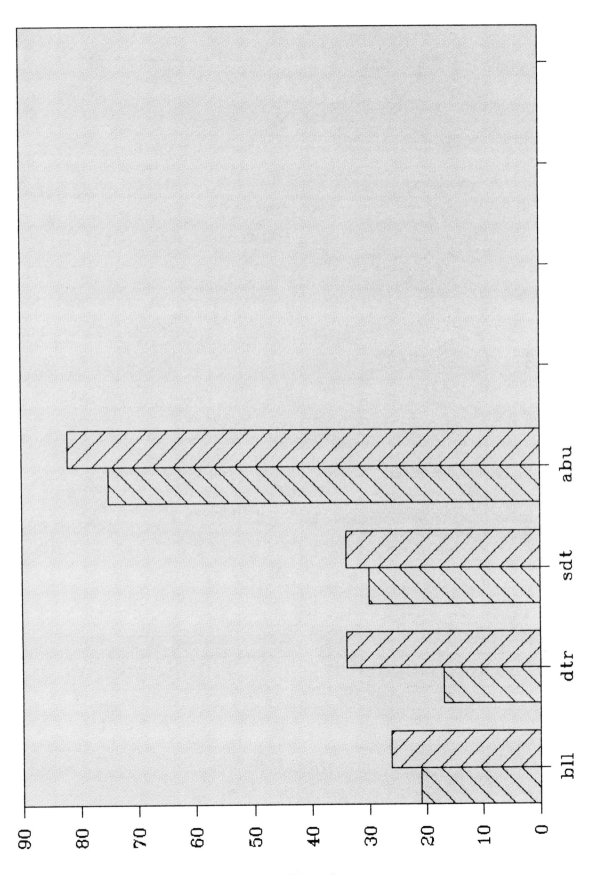

Figure 6

\015	sets an Epson printer to compressed font
RETURN	accepts setup and displays options
M	selects Margin option
R	selects Right option
230	characters per line
RETURN	displays options
Q	selects Quit option and returns to main print menu
R	displays Range to print from
.	ellipsis—indicates from-to

Move cursor, with arrow keys, to last coordinate in area you wish to print. The screen will reverse to indicate the area being printed.

RETURN	executes the command
G	selects Go option and prints

To exit out of PRINT command, type:

Q	selects Quit option and exits out of PRINT command

Now you will exit from the program and load the Graphics program. To do this, place your 1-2-3 Systems Disk in Drive 1 (or A).

Then type:

/Q	exits out of program
Y	yes, to confirm

PRINTING THE GRAPH

Then you will remove the 1-2-3 systems disk and replace it with the Graphic program disk. Then type:

G	selects GRAPHIC option
S	selects Select option

Place your cursor on name of graph to be selected by using the space bar.

Place your cursor on Ticker, using the space bar.

RETURN	selects Ticker as picture to be graphed
O	selects options
C	selects Color option
G	selects Grid to color
B	selects Black option
A	selects A to color
B	selects Black option
B	selects B to color
B	selects Black option
Q	quits color option
F	selects Font option
1	selects Font 1

Move your cursor to Font desired and then hit space bar to mark Font selection. In this exercise we will select Roman 1. Place the cursor on Roman1 and press space bar.

RETURN	selects Roman1
S	selects Size option
F	selects Full option
Q	quits Size option
Q	quits Options option
G	selects Go option

Your graph should now be being printed out on your Epson. For other printers and plotters, refer to your manuals.

After printing is done, remove your Graphics program disk and replace it with your 1-2-3 systems disk. Then type:

Q	quits Graphics
Y	Yes, to confirm
RETURN	returns you to main program

Now to show you just how quick and easy it is to do a data query and graph, you will want to load back in the Stock Portfolio Worksheet and we will then change our data criteria and graph it.

Load your worksheet back into memory. Type:

/F   starts FILE command

R   selects Retrieve option

Place your cursor on file name and press:

RETURN   executes the command

MAKING NEW CRITERIA ENTRIES

Put in new formulas for Criteria.

We will change the Criteria formulas to select all stocks with a loss. To do this we will erase the formula in the shares column and change the formula in the Gains $ column to select stocks that have no loss.

To erase the formula in the Shares columns place your cursor on A20 and type:

/R   starts RANGE command

E   selects Erase option and displays
                                        Range to erase: A20..A20

RETURN   executes the command

Now edit the formula in Gain $. Place your cursor on B20 and press:

F2 (edit key)   displays the formula to be edited

Move your cursor beneath the ˃ sign and press the Delete key. Then type in ˂ sign. (+ H5 ˂ 0)

RETURN   enters the new formula

Press your F7 key (Query) which will then display stocks with a loss in the Output Range, as illustrated in Figure 7.

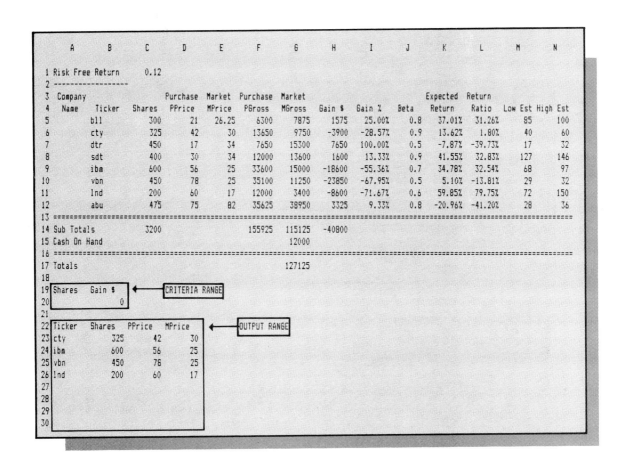

	A	B	C	D	E	F	G	H	I	J	K	L	M	N
1	Risk Free Return		0.12											
2	------------------													
3	Company			Purchase	Market	Purchase	Market				Expected	Return		
4	Name	Ticker	Shares	PPrice	MPrice	PGross	MGross	Gain $	Gain %	Beta	Return	Ratio	Low Est	High Est
5		bll	300	21	26.25	6300	7875	1575	25.00%	0.8	37.01%	31.26%	85	100
6		cty	325	42	30	13650	9750	-3900	-28.57%	0.9	13.62%	1.80%	40	60
7		dtr	450	17	34	7650	15300	7650	100.00%	0.5	-7.87%	-39.73%	17	32
8		sdt	400	30	34	12000	13600	1600	13.33%	0.9	41.55%	32.83%	127	146
9		ibm	600	56	25	33600	15000	-18600	-55.36%	0.7	34.78%	32.54%	68	97
10		vbn	450	78	25	35100	11250	-23850	-67.95%	0.5	5.10%	-13.81%	29	32
11		lnd	200	60	17	12000	3400	-8600	-71.67%	0.6	59.85%	79.75%	72	150
12		abu	475	75	82	35625	38950	3325	9.33%	0.8	-20.96%	-41.20%	28	36
13	===
14	Sub Totals		3200			155925	115125	-40800						
15	Cash On Hand						12000							
16	===
17	Totals						127125							
18														

19	Shares	Gain $	← CRITERIA RANGE
20		0	
21			

22	Ticker	Shares	PPrice	MPrice	← OUTPUT RANGE
23	cty	325	42	30	
24	ibm	600	56	25	
25	vbn	450	78	25	
26	lnd	200	60	17	
27					
28					
29					
30					

Figure 7

Then press F10 key to graph the data which will be displayed on the CRT, as illustrated in Figure 8.

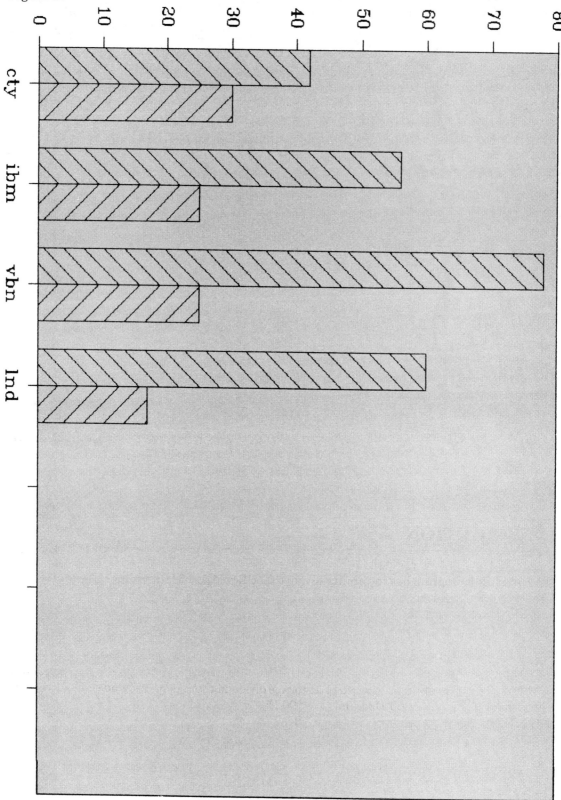

Figure 8

EXERCISE TWO

ACCOUNTS RECEIVABLE AGEING REPORT

DESCRIPTION

The Lotus 1-2-3 program has the ability to move specific blocks of data to disk storage and then reenter those blocks back onto the worksheet in a different area. 1-2-3 allows us to do this in a single keystroke with the use of Keyboard Macros. This technique has been used in this exercise to demonstrate the ability to update record information.

To demonstrate these capabilities, an Accounts Receivable Ageing worksheet has been set up. To age the accounts listed, an updating operation is performed once a month. Current accounts and those over 30 days old are moved to a storage disk and then reentered and repositioned on the worksheet. The Over 60 Day and Over 90 Day values are moved to a storage disk, then reentered in a Work Area for an accumulating function.

OPERATIONS PERFORMED

Setting Up The Worksheet Format

Entering Mathematical Formulas

Naming Groups of Coordinates

Making Worksheet Entries

Worksheet Updating

Making Monthly Entries

Updating the Worksheet Using the Keyboard Macros

Saving

Printing

FUNCTIONS USED

@SUM

COMMANDS USED

COPY	copies formulas
FILE	saves values
FILE	moves
FILE	saves worksheet
PRINT	prints worksheet
RANGE	centers labels
RANGE	names coordinates
RANGE	erases
REPEAT	repeats dashed lines
WORKSHEET	adjusts column width
WORKSHEET	formats in currency

SETTING UP THE WORKSHEET FORMAT

Using the following directions, set up your worksheet by copying Figure 1 exactly as it is illustrated, retaining exact row and column locations of all information.

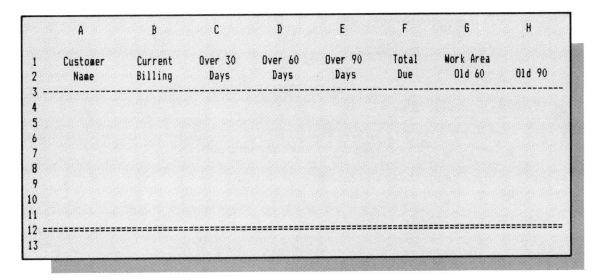

	A	B	C	D	E	F	G	H
1	Customer	Current	Over 30	Over 60	Over 90	Total	Work Area	
2	Name	Billing	Days	Days	Days	Due	Old 60	Old 90
3	----							
4								
5								
6								
7								
8								
9								
10								
11								
12	====							
13								

Figure 1

Enter your column headings.

After entering your column headings, you will center them in the columns by using the Center option.

Place your cursor on A1 and type:

/R	starts RANGE command
L	selects Label-Prefix option
C	selects Center option and displays Range of labels A1..A1

Move your cursor to H2 with the arrow keys. Notice the screen is reversing to show you which coordinates are to be formatted.

RETURN	executes the command

You will also want to widen all the column widths to accommodate numbers larger than 9 digits, which is the default when you load in the worksheet. Type:

/W	starts WORKSHEET command
G	selects Global option
C	selects Column-Width option
12	number of spaces in column
RETURN	executes the command

On this worksheet you will want to expand column A to allow for a longer than a 12-space customer name. To expand the width of column A,

Place your cursor on column A and type:

/W	starts WORKSHEET command
C	selects Column-Width option
S	selects Set option and displays column width
16	number of spaces in column
RETURN	executes the command

To enter dashed lines on your worksheet, place your cursor on the left-most column of the row where you want the line (A3 in this example.) Type:

\	starts REPEAT command
—	label to be repeated
RETURN	executes the command

The column your cursor is on will now have a line of dashes across its width. To extend the dashed line in the same row across the remaining columns, leave your cursor where it is and type:

/C	starts COPY command and displays Range to copy from

RETURN	displays Range to copy to
B3	first coordinate to copy to
•	ellipsis—indicates from-to
H3	last coordinate to copy to
RETURN	executes the command

The dashed line will now appear extended across the columns you have indicated by your coordinates. To enter a double-dashed line on the worksheet, repeat the operations above, using the symbol = as your label to be repeated.

To format all locations to display value entries in dollars and cents, type:

/W	starts WORKSHEET command
G	selects Global option
F	selects Format option
C	selects Currency option and displays number of decimal places: 2
RETURN	executes the command

ENTERING MATHEMATICAL FORMULAS

You will now begin entering mathematical formulas that will establish the relationships between column and row positions. The formulas and their locations are illustrated in Figure 2.

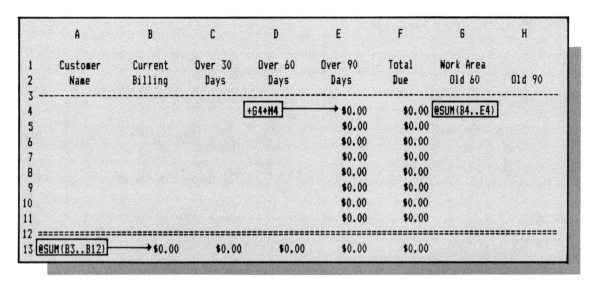

Figure 2

Formula one will add the values in the Current Billing column.

Place your cursor on B13 and type:

@SUM(	adds values in the list
B3	first coordinate of column to add
•	ellipsis—indicates from-to
B12)	last coordinate of column to add
RETURN	enters the formula

Your next operation is to copy the formula just entered at the bottom of each column you wish to add.

Leave your cursor on B13 and type:

/C	starts COPY command and displays Range to copy from
RETURN	displays Range to copy to
C13	first coordinate to copy to
•	ellipsis—indicates from-to
F13	last coordinate to copy to
RETURN	executes the command

Formula two, in the Over 90 Days column, will add the values in the two Work Area columns, and display the answer in the Over 90 Days column. This value will reflect the accumulated value of accounts receivable held more than 90 days.

Place your cursor on E4 and type:

+	prepares coordinate to accept a numeric expression
G4	coordinate containing Old 60, Work Area
+	adds
H4	coordinate containing Old 90, Work Area
RETURN	enters the formula

Formula three, in the Total Due column, adds the sum of the values in each column in the row to the left.

Place your cursor on F4 and type:

@SUM(	adds values in the list
B4	first coordinate of row to add
.	ellipsis—indicates from-to
E4)	last coordinate of row to add
RETURN	enters the formula

It will now be necessary to copy the two formulas just entered into each row in their respective columns (Over 90 Days and Total Due).
Place your cursor on E4 and type:

/C	starts COPY command and displays Range to copy from
E4	first coordinate to copy from
.	ellipsis—indicates from-to
F4	last coordinate to copy from
RETURN	displays Range to copy to
E5	first coordinate to copy to
.	ellipsis—indicates from-to
E11	last coordinate to copy to
RETURN	executes the command

NAMING GROUPS OF COORDINATES

Now that the formulas are entered, we will want to name certain columns to be used later for updating purposes. We will first name the columns Current Billing and Over 30 Days, as BILLING. To do this,

Place your cursor on B4 and type:

/R	starts RANGE command
N	selects Name option
C	selects Create option

BILLING	name
RETURN	displays Enter Range: B4..B4

Move your cursor to C11 with the arrow keys.

The screen will reverse to show you which coordinate locations are being named.

RETURN	executes the command

The next set of locations to be named will be the Over 60 Days and Over 90 Days columns, as OVER60.

Place your cursor on D4 and type:

/R	starts RANGE command
N	selects Name option
C	selects Create option
OVER60	name
RETURN	displays Enter Range: D4..D4

Move your cursor to E11 with the arrow keys. The screen will reverse to show you which coordinates are being named.

RETURN	executes the command

MAKING WORKSHEET ENTRIES

Your Accounts Receivable Ageing Worksheet is now set up. Once a month, all you have to do is perform the update process, described in the next section, and make current billing entries. To perform the following series of exercises, type in the entries illustrated in Figure 3. For this example, entries have been selected to illustrate a worksheet in operation for more than 90 Days.

NOTE

Do not type in the Over 90 Days column. The value to be shown in the Over 90 Days column should be typed in the adjacent row of the Old 90 column in the Work Area. It will be displayed in the Over 90 Days column by the formula entered there.

Never enter values in coordinates containing formulas, or the formulas will be erased.

	A	B	C	D	E	F	G	H
1	Customer	Current	Over 30	Over 60	Over 90	Total	Work Area	
2	Name	Billing	Days	Days	Days	Due	Old 60	Old 90
3	---
4	Sitco Co.		$45.00		$0.00	$45.00		
5	Phillips Co.			$25.00	$45.00	$70.00		$45.00
6	Williams Co.		$56.58		$0.00	$56.58		
7	Steinway Co.				$89.00	$89.00		$89.00
8	Knoll Co.			$35.00	$0.00	$35.00		
9	Pine Co.	$75.16			$15.00	$90.16		$15.00
10	Anderson Co.	$84.00			$0.00	$84.00		
11	Morse Co.	$3,578.00			$0.00	$3,578.00		
12	===
13		$3,737.16	$101.58	$60.00	$149.00	$4,047.74		

Figure 3

WORKSHEET UPDATING

To update the worksheet, you will first save, using the Xtract option in the file command to save the columns named BILLING and OVER60 out onto your data disk. You will then move these columns back onto the worksheet in their new locations. Then you will blank the Current Billing columns which will complete the updating process, and your worksheet will be ready for your new month's entries.

First you will save the columns named BILLING, which are Current Billing and Over 30 Days. To do this, type:

/F	starts FILE command
X	selects Xtract option
V	selects Value option which saves only the values
BILLING	filename
RETURN	displays Range

BILLING	name of columns
RETURN	executes the command

The next operation will be to save the columns named OVER60, which are Over 60 Days and Over 90 Days. To do this, type:

/F	starts FILE command
X	selects Xtract option
V	selects Value option which saves only the values
OVER60	filename
RETURN	displays Range
OVER60	name of columns
RETURN	executes the command

You will need to move these files back onto your worksheet in their new updated locations.

First you will need to erase all the information in the Current Billing columns through the Over 60 Days columns and the information in the Work Area columns. To do this quickly and easily, we will name the Current Billing through the Over 60 Days columns CURRENT, and the Work Area columns WORKAREA.

Place your cursor on B4 and type:

/R	starts RANGE command
N	selects Name option
C	selects Create option
CURRENT	name of coordinates
RETURN	displays Range: B4..B4

Move your cursor to D11, with the arrow keys. The screen will reverse to show you which coordinates are being named.

RETURN	executes the command

Next we will name the Work Area columns.

Place your cursor on G4 and type:

/R	starts RANGE command
N	selects Name option

C	selects Create option
WORKAREA	name of coordinates
RETURN	displays Range: G4..G4

Move your cursor to H11, with the arrow keys. The screen will reverse to show you which coordinates are being named.

RETURN	executes the command

The next operation is to erase the Current Billing through Over 60 Days columns and the work Area columns before reloading the files back onto the Work Area. Type:

/R	starts RANGE command
E	selects Erase option
CURRENT	name of coordinates
RETURN	executes the command

Next operation is to erase the Work Area columns. Type:

/R	starts RANGE command
E	selects Erase option
WORKAREA	name of coordinates
RETURN	executes the command

Now we will move the BILLING file into the Over 30 Days column, which will place the Current Billing information in the Over 30 Days column, and the Over 30 Days information into the Over 60 Days column.

Place your cursor on C4 and type:

/F	starts FILE command
C	selects Combine option
C	selects Copy option
E	selects Entire File option
BILLING	filename
RETURN	executes the command

Next we will load in the OVER60 file into the Work Area, which places the Over 60 Days information into the Old 60 column, and places the Over 90 Days information in the Old 90 column.

Place your cursor on G4 and type:

/F	starts FILE command
C	selects Combine option
C	selects Copy option
E	selects Entire File option
OVER60	filename
RETURN	executes the command

Your worksheet should look like Figure 4.

	A	B	C	D	E	F	G	H
1	Customer	Current	Over 30	Over 60	Over 90	Total	Work Area	
2	Name	Billing	Days	Days	Days	Due	Old 60	Old 90
3	----	----	----	----	----	----	----	----
4	Sitco Co.			$45.00	$0.00	$45.00		$0.00
5	Phillips Co.				$70.00	$70.00	$25.00	$45.00
6	Williams Co.			$56.58	$0.00	$56.58		$0.00
7	Steinway Co.				$89.00	$89.00		$89.00
8	Knoll Co.				$35.00	$35.00	$35.00	$0.00
9	Pine Co.		$75.16		$15.00	$90.16		$15.00
10	Anderson Co.		$84.00		$0.00	$84.00		$0.00
11	Morse Co.		$3,578.00		$0.00	$3,578.00		$0.00
12	=====	=====	=====	=====	=====	=====	=====	=====
13		$0.00	$3,737.16	$101.58	$209.00	$4,047.74		

Figure 4

MAKING MONTHLY ENTRIES

Monthly worksheet entries will take one of two forms: current billings and payments.

To make current billing entries, type them directly into the Current Billings column. To make a payment entry into the Over 30 Days or the Over 60 Days columns, place your cursor on the value you wish to deduct from, and

Press:

F2	edit function key which displays the value in that location
—	subtracts

Type in payment value.

RETURN	enters the value

To make over 90 days payments, place your cursor on the appropriate value in the Work Area, Old 60 or Old 90 columns. Proceed as described above, using the edit function key (F2).

UPDATING USING THE KEYBOARD MACROS

1-2-3 has an extremely powerful feature called Keyboard Macros, which allows you to set up a string of keystroke information in a small file, enabling you to perform an operation, such as the LEDGER UPDATING we just did, with a single keystroke.

To set up the Keyboard Macros, you will first need to enter the keystroke information into a coordinate or a group of adjacent coordinates in a column.

Next you will need to name the coordinate or group of coordinates which contain the keystroke information, using a backslash followed by any single character from A to Z. Example: \A.

First we will enter the Keyboard Macros file.

────────────────────────── **NOTE** ──────────────────────────

An apostrophe (') is entered at the beginning of each line to prepare coordinates for label information.

The ˜ represents a RETURN.

We have put an r after the filename RETURN because the computer asks if you want to Replace or Cancel a file which already exists on the disk. The r represents the Replace.

{goto} moves cursor to the coordinate following it.

──

Place your cursor on A17, and type:

```
'/fxvBILLING~BILLING~r
'/fxvover60~over60~r
'/recurrent~
'/reworkarea~
'{goto}c4~
'/fccebilling~
'{goto}g4~
'/fcceover60~
```

Second operation will be to name the coordinates containing the Keyboard Macros.

Place your cursor on A17 and type:

/R	starts RANGE command
N	selects Name option
C	selects Create option
\ A	name of coordinate
RETURN	displays Range: A17..A17

Move your cursor to A24.

RETURN	executes the command

Next enter current billing information. Your worksheet should look like Figure 5.

	A	B	C	D	E	F	G	H
1	Customer	Current	Over 30	Over 60	Over 90	Total	Work Area	
2	Name	Billing	Days	Days	Days	Due	Old 60	Old 90
3	------	-------	-------	-------	-------	-------	-------	-------
4	Sitco Co.	$100.00	$30.00		$0.00	$130.00		$0.00
5	Phillips Co.				$70.00	$70.00	$25.00	$45.00
6	Williams Co.		$25.00		$0.00	$25.00		$0.00
7	Steinway Co.	$85.00			$89.00	$174.00		$89.00
8	Knoll Co.				$35.00	$35.00	$35.00	$0.00
9	Pine Co.	$125.00	$50.00	$75.16	$15.00	$265.16		$15.00
10	Anderson Co.		$50.00	$84.00	$0.00	$134.00		$0.00
11	Morse Co.			$3,578.00	$0.00	$3,578.00		$0.00
12	==========	========	========	========	========	========	========	========
13		$310.00	$155.00	$3,737.16	$209.00	$4,411.16		
14								
15								
16								
17	/fxvbilling~billing~r							
18	/fxvover60~over60~r							
19	/recurrent~							
20	/reworkarea~							
21	{goto}c4~							
22	/fccebilling~							
23	{goto}g4~							
24	/fcceover60~							

Figure 5

Now that the keyboard macros file is named, to demonstrate its use, and, to execute the macros, hold the Alt key down and press A. Sit back and watch what happens.

Your worksheet should look like Figure 6.

	A	B	C	D	E	F	G	H
1	Customer	Current	Over 30	Over 60	Over 90	Total	Work Area	
2	Name	Billing	Days	Days	Days	Due	Old 60	Old 90
3	--							
4	Sitco Co.		$100.00	$30.00	$0.00	$130.00		$0.00
5	Phillips Co.				$70.00	$70.00		$70.00
6	Williams Co.			$25.00	$0.00	$25.00		$0.00
7	Steinway Co.		$85.00		$89.00	$174.00		$89.00
8	Knoll Co.				$35.00	$35.00		$35.00
9	Pine Co.		$125.00	$50.00	$90.16	$265.16	$75.16	$15.00
10	Anderson Co.			$50.00	$84.00	$134.00	$84.00	$0.00
11	Morse Co.				$3,578.00	$3,578.00	$3,578.00	$0.00
12	==							
13		$0.00	$310.00	$155.00	$3,946.16	$4,411.16		
14								
15								
16								
17	/fxvbilling~billing~r							
18	/fxvover60~over60~r							
19	/recurrent~							
20	/reworkarea~							
21	{goto}c4~							
22	/fccebilling~							
23	{goto}g4~							
24	/fcceover60~							

Figure 6

SAVING

You may wish to save your entire worksheet. To do this leave your cursor on any location and type:

/F   starts FILE command

S   selects SAVE option

Type in name of file. Do not leave spaces between words.

RETURN   executes the command

PRINTING

To print out all or a portion of your worksheet, use the following directions, which are given for the Epson printer (compressed font).

Place your cursor on A1 and type:

/P	starts PRINT command
P	displays options
O	selects Options option
S	selects Setup option and displays Enter Setup String
\ 015	sets an Epson printer to compressed font
RETURN	accepts setup and displays options
M	selects Margin option
R	selects Right option
230	characters per line
RETURN	displays options
Q	selects Quit option and returns to main print menu
R	displays Range to print from
.	ellipsis—indicates from-to

Move cursor, with arrow keys, to last coordinate in area you wish to print. The screen will reverse to indicate the area being printed.

RETURN	executes the command
G	selects Go option and prints

To exit out of PRINT command, type:

Q	selects Quit option and exits out of PRINT command

EXERCISE THREE

ACCOUNTS PAYABLE

DESCRIPTION

The Lotus 1-2-3 program has a powerful Date function which allows us to calculate and display dates.

To demonstrate this ability, an accounts payable worksheet has been set up, which determines on which date to pay an invoice to receive a discount, and calculates the amount of savings if the discount is taken.

OPERATIONS PERFORMED

Setting Up The Worksheet Format

Entering Mathematical Formulas

Making Worksheet Entries

Saving

Printing

FUNCTIONS USED

DATE
SUM

COMMANDS USED

COPY	copies formulas
FILE	saves worksheet
PRINT	prints worksheet
RANGE	centers labels
RANGE	formats in 2 decimal places
RANGE	formats in Date format
REPEAT	repeats dashed lines
WORKSHEET	adjusts column width

SETTING UP THE WORKSHEET FORMAT

Using the following directions, set up and label the exercise format on your worksheet, copying Figure 1 exactly as it is illustrated, retaining exact row and column locations of all information.

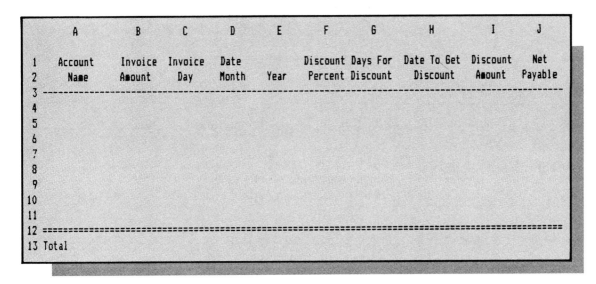

	A	B	C	D	E	F	G	H	I	J
1	Account	Invoice	Invoice	Date		Discount	Days For	Date To Get	Discount	Net
2	Name	Amount	Day	Month	Year	Percent	Discount	Discount	Amount	Payable
3	--
4										
5										
6										
7										
8										
9										
10										
11										
12	==
13	Total									

Figure 1

For this exercise we need to make columns A & H wider than the default, which is 9.

To expand column A, place your cursor on column A and type:

/W	starts WORKSHEET Command
C	selects Column-Width option
S	selects Set option and displays column width
14	number of spaces in column
RETURN	executes the command

To expand column H, place your cursor on column H and type:

/W	starts WORKSHEET command
C	selects Column-Width option
S	selects Set option and displays column width
14	number of spaces in column
RETURN	executes the command

Enter your column headings.

After entering your column headings, you will center them in the columns by using the Center option.

Place your cursor on A1 and type:

/R	starts RANGE command
L	selects Label-Prefix option
C	selects Center option and displays Range of labels A1..A1

Move your cursor to J2. Notice the screen is reversing to show you which coordinates are to be formatted.

RETURN	executes the command

To enter dashed lines on your worksheet, place your cursor on the left-most column of the row where you want the line (A3 in this example.) Type:

\	starts REPEAT command
—	label to be repeated
RETURN	executes the command

The column your cursor is on will now have a line of dashes across its width. To extend the dashed line in the same row across the remaining columns, leave your cursor where it is and type:

/C	starts COPY command and displays Range to copy from
RETURN	displays Range to copy to
B3	first coordinate to copy to

•   ellipsis—indicates from-to

J3   last coordinate to copy to

RETURN   executes the command

The dashed line will now appear extended across the columns you have indicated by your coordinates. To enter a double-dashed line on the worksheet, repeat the operations above, using the symbol = as your label to be repeated.

Column B needs to be formatted to display two decimal places.

Place your cursor on B4 and type:

/R   starts RANGE command

F   selects Format option

F   selects Fixed option and displays number of decimal places: 2

RETURN   displays Range to format B4..B4

Move your cursor to B13 with arrow keys. Screen will reverse to show area being formatted.

RETURN   executes the command

ENTERING MATHEMATICAL FORMULAS

You will now begin entering mathematical formulas that will establish the relationship between column and row positions. The formulas and their positions are illustrated in Fig. 2.

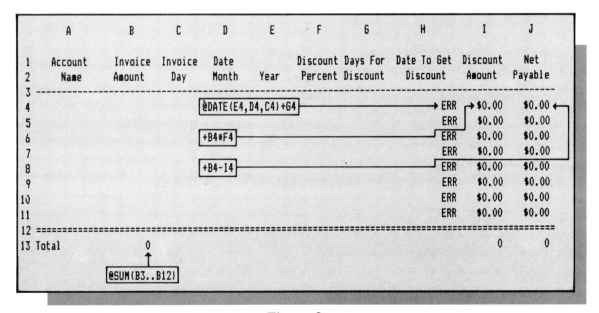

Figure 2

Formula one, in the Date to Get Discount column, uses the Date function which generates an absolute number which identifies the Invoice Date. We then add to that number the Days To Get Discount. That number is then formatted to display the day, month and year.

Place your cursor on H4 and type:

@DATE(	starts DATE function
E4,	coordinate containing Year
D4,	coordinate containing Month
C4)	coordinate containing Day
+	adds
G4	coordinate containing Days for Discount
RETURN	enters the formula

To format the number to read in day, month and year format, leave your cursor on H4 and type:

/R	starts RANGE command
F	selects Format option
D	selects Date format
1	selects (DD-MMM-YY) and displays Range to format
RETURN	executes the command

Formula two, in the Discount Amount column, multiplies the Invoice Amount by Discount Percent, and will display it in Currency format.

Place your cursor on I4 and type:

+	prepares coordinate to accept a numeric expression
B4	coordinate containing Invoice Amount
*	multiplies
F4	coordinate containing Discount Percent
RETURN	enters the formula

/R	starts RANGE command
F	selects Format option
C	selects Currency format and displays decimal places: 2
RETURN	range to format: I4..I4
RETURN	executes the command

Formula three, in the Net Payable column, subtracts the Discount Amount from Invoice Amount, and it will be formatted in Currency format.

Place your cursor on J4 and type:

+B4	coordinate containing Invoice Amount
—	subtracts
I4	coordinate containing Discount Amount
RETURN	enters the formula
/R	starts RANGE command
F	selects Format option
C	selects Currency option and displays decimal places: 2
RETURN	range to format J4..J4
RETURN	executes the command

The next operation will be to copy the three formulas just entered down their appropriate columns.

Place your cursor on H4 and type:

/C	starts COPY command and displays Range to copy from: H4..H4

Move your cursor to J4 with the arrow keys. The screen will reverse to show you which coordinates are being copied.

RETURN	displays Range to copy to

Move your cursor to H5, with the arrow keys

.	ellipsis—indicates from-to

Move your cursor to H11, with the arrow keys. The screen will reverse to show you which coordinate are being copied into.

RETURN	executes the command

———————————————— **NOTE** ————————————————

In the Date to Get Discount column, ERR will appear until an invoice date is entered.

Formula four, in the Invoice Amount column, Total row, sums the column, including the single and double dashed lines. The single and double dashed lines are included in the formula so that later, when you wish to add new rows, they will be included.

Place your cursor on B13 and type:

@SUM(	adds values in following list
B3	first value in list
•	ellipsis—indicates from-to
B12)	last value in list
RETURN	enters the formula

Next operation is to copy the formula just entered into the Discount Amount and Net Payable columns. To do this,

Leave your cursor on B13 and type:

/C	starts COPY command and displays range to copy from
RETURN	displays Range to copy to
I13	first cell to copy to
•	ellipsis—indicates from-to
J13	last cell to copy to
RETURN	executes the command

MAKING WORKSHEET ENTRIES

Now make worksheet entries as illustrated in Figure 3.

	A	B	C	D	E	F	G	H	I	J
1	Account	Invoice	Invoice	Date		Discount	Days For	Date To Get	Discount	Net
2	Name	Amount	Day	Month	Year	Percent	Discount	Discount	Amount	Payable
3	-----	-----	-----	-----	-----	-----	-----	-----	-----	-----
4	Rudolph Co	500.00	30	12	83	0.02	10	09-Jan-84	$10.00	$490.00
5	Acme Co	225.00	19	10	83	0.02	10	29-Oct-83	$4.50	$220.50
6	Industrial Co	336.00	18	3	83	0.05	45	02-May-83	$16.80	$319.20
7	Training Corp	778.48	2	7	83	0.05	45	16-Aug-83	$38.92	$739.56
8	Cleveland Co	472.00	15	4	83	0.08	14	29-Apr-83	$37.76	$434.24
9	Central Co	988.43	7	11	83	0.02	10	17-Nov-83	$19.77	$968.66
10	Anderson	634.00	29	9	83	0.05	45	13-Nov-83	$31.70	$602.30
11	Safety Corp	100.00	9	5	83	0.08	14	23-May-83	$8.00	$92.00
12	=====	=====	=====	=====	=====	=====	=====	=====	=====	=====
13	Total	4033.91							167.4526	3866.457

Figure 3

SAVING

You may wish to save your entire worksheet. To do this leave your cursor on any location and type:

/F	starts FILE command
S	selects SAVE option

Type in name of file. Do not leave spaces between words.

RETURN	executes the command

PRINTING

To print out all or a portion of your worksheet, use the following directions, which are given for the Epson printer (compressed font).

Place your cursor on A1 and type:

/P	starts PRINT command
P	displays options
O	selects Options option

S	selects Setup option and displays Enter Setup String
\015	sets an Epson printer to compressed font
RETURN	accepts setup and displays options
M	selects Margin option
R	selects Right option
230	characters per line
RETURN	displays options
Q	selects Quit option and returns to main print menu
R	displays Range to print from
•	ellipsis—indicates from-to

Move cursor, with arrow keys, to last coordinate in area you wish to print. The screen will reverse to indicate the area being printed.

RETURN	executes the command
G	selects Go option and prints

To exit out of PRINT command, type:

Q	selects Quit option and exits out of PRINT command

EXERCISE FOUR

ESTIMATING

DESCRIPTION

The Lotus 1-2-3 program allows you to set up tables of information, enabling you to select values from the tables and then use those values in formulas.

To demonstrate this, a manufacturing estimating worksheet has been designed for a pipe manufacturer, which enters a set of criteria: size parameters, quantity and material grade for a particular pipe. Then the estimating sheet takes this set of criteria and looks up the appropriate values in tables to determine the proper machine to use, the cost of material required, the manufacturing time and cost, and then determines the total job cost.

OPERATIONS PERFORMED

Setting Up The Worksheet Format

Naming Tables

Entering Mathematical Formulas

Entering Parameters

Making Additional Entries

Saving

Printing

FUNCTIONS USED

IF
INT
LOOKUP
SUM

COMMANDS USED

COPY	copies formulas
FILE	saves worksheet
PRINT	prints worksheet
RANGE	names coordinates
RANGE	formats in currency
REPEAT	repeats dashed lines

SETTING UP THE WORKSHEET FORMAT

To set up your estimating sheet, use the following directions, copying Figure 1 exactly as it is illustrated, retaining exact row and column locations of all information.

Enter your column headings.

To enter dashed lines on your worksheet, place your cursor on the left-most column of the row where you want the line (A15 in this example.)

Type:

\	starts REPEAT command
—	label to be repeated
RETURN	executes the command

The column your cursor is on will now have a line of dashes across its width. To extend the dashed line in the same row across the next column, leave your cursor where it is and type:

/C	starts COPY command and displays Range to copy from
RETURN	displays Range to copy to
B15	first coordinate to copy to
.	ellipsis—indicates from-to
B15	last coordinate to copy to
RETURN	executes the command

The dashed line will now appear extended across the columns you have indicated by your coordinates. To enter a double-dashed line on the worksheet, repeat the operations above, using the symbol = as your label to be repeated.

Column C needs to be expanded. To expand column C,

Place your cursor on C1 and type:

/W	starts WORKSHEET command
C	selects Column-Width option
S	selects Set option and displays column width

```
       A       B       C       D       E       F       G       H       I

 1 Material Grade:
 2 Quantity:
 3 Length,Feet:
 4 Diameter, Inch
 5
 6 Machine To Use:
 7 Total SqFt Needed:
 8 Manufacture Time
 9 Manufacturing Cost:
10 Material Cost:
11                     =========
12 Total Job Cost
13
14 Table1                   Table2                   Table3
15 -------------------      Machine To Use           Machine To Use
16        1       4         Diameter Machine #       Length   Machine #
17        2       5         -------------------      -------------------
18                                1       1                 0       4
19                                2       2                20       5
20                                3       3                25       6
21                                4       4
22                                5       7
23
24 Table4                        Table5                   Table6
25 Hrly Machine Cost             Markup Percentage        Mat'l Grade Cost
26 & Production Rate             Quantity Percent         Material Cost/SqFt
27 Machine # Price/Hr SqFt/Hr    -------------------      -------------------
28 --------------------------          0      2.5              100     5.75
29        1      25.55     36         100      2.25            150     4.85
30        2      30.55     45         300      1.75            200     3.79
31        3      20.25     50         500      1.5             250     5.55
32        4      45.55     60        1000      1.25            300     6.75
33        5      56.85     45
34        6      18.55     25
35        7     125.55     75
```

Figure 1

12	number of spaces in column
RETURN	executes the command

NAMING TABLES

Before entering mathematical formulas you will want to name the tables so they will be easily used in the upcoming formulas.

We will name the tables 1 through 6.

First table to be named is Table 1.

Place your cursor on A16 and type:

/R	starts RANGE command
N	selects Name option
C	selects Create option
TABLE1	name
RETURN	displays Range A16..A16

Move your cursor to B17 with the arrow keys. The screen will reverse to show the coordinates being named.

RETURN	executes the command

Second table to be named is Table 2, Machine to Use.

Place your cursor on D18 and type:

/R	starts RANGE command
N	selects Name option
C	selects Create option
TABLE2	name
RETURN	displays Range D18..D18

Move your cursor to E22 with the arrow keys. The screen will reverse to show the coordinates being named.

RETURN	executes the command

Third table to be named is Table 3, Machine to Use.

Place your cursor on G18 and type:

/R	starts RANGE command

N	selects Name option
C	selects Create option
TABLE3	name
RETURN	displays Range G18..G18

Move your cursor to H20 with the arrow keys. The screen will reverse to show the coordinates being named.

RETURN	executes the command

Fourth table to be named is Table 4, Hrly Machine Cost & Production Rate.

Place your cursor on A29 and type:

/R	starts RANGE command
N	selects Name option
C	selects Create option
TABLE4	name
RETURN	displays Range A29..A29

Move your cursor to C35 with the arrow keys. The screen will reverse to show the coordinates being named.

RETURN	executes the command

Fifth table to be named is Table 5, Markup Percentage.

Place your cursor on E28 and type:

/R	starts RANGE command
N	selects Name option
C	selects Create option
TABLE5	name
RETURN	displays Range E28..E28

Move your cursor to F32 with the arrow keys. The screen will reverse to show the coordinates being named.

RETURN	executes the command

Sixth table to be named is Table 6, Mat'l Grade Cost.

Place your cursor on H28 and type:

/R	starts RANGE command
N	selects Name option
C	selects Create option
TABLE6	name
RETURN	displays Range H28..H28

Move your cursor to I32 with the arrow keys. The screen will reverse to show the coordinates being named.

RETURN	executes the command

ENTERING MATHEMATICAL FORMULAS

You will now begin entering mathematical formulas that will establish the relationships between column and row positions. The formulas and their positions are illustrated in Figure 2.

Formula one, in Table 1, to the immediate right of 1, determines the machine to use according to the diameter size.

NOTE

All tables in this exercise are in a vertical format, which means the tables are in column format. The left-most column of the table is considered the labels of the table, and the adjacent columns to the right contain the values. The second column of the table is considered as the first offset. The third column of the table is considered as the second offset, and etc. LOOKUP function being used will be indicated by @VLOOKUP.

If the tables were in a horizontal format, or row format, the top-most row would be the labels, and the rows beneath it would be the values, the second row being the first offset, etc. The LOOKUP function being used would be indicated by @HLOOKUP.

Place your cursor on B16 and type:

@VLOOKUP(	starts LOOKUP function
C4,	coordinate containing Diameter value to look up
TABLE2,	name of range
1)	first offset

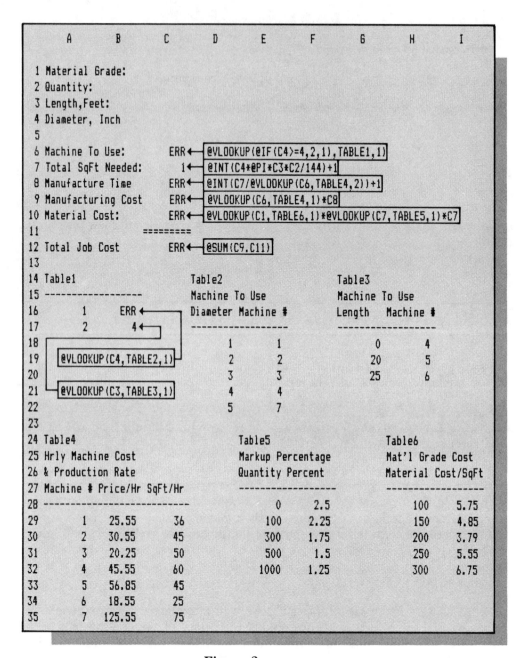

Figure 2

RETURN   enters the formula

Formula two, in Table 1, to the immediate right of 2, determines the machine to be used according to the length.

Place your cursor on B17 and type:

@VLOOKUP(starts LOOKUP function

C3,   coordinate containing Length,
                                value to look up

TABLE3,   name of range

1)   first offset

RETURN   enters the formula

Formula three, to the immediate right of Machine to Use, uses an IF function to determine the value to look up in Table 1. The value that it looks up in Table 1 will be the machine number to use. The IF function says if C4, the Diameter, is greater than or equal to 4, it will give a value of 2. If C4, the Diameter, is not greater than or equal to 4, it will give a value of one. This value is then used to determine the value to be looked up from Table 1.

Place your cursor on C6 and type:

@VLOOKUP(starts LOOKUP function

@IF(starts IF function

C4   coordinate containing diameter

> =   logical operators

4,   value to compare against

2,   selected if comparison is TRUE

1),   selected if comparison is FALSE

TABLE1,   name of Range

1)   first offset

RETURN   enters formula

Formula four, to the immediate right of Total SqFt Needed, calculates the amount of flat material required to manufacture the pipe by first determining the pipe circumference in inches by multiplying the diameter times PI (3.1415926536). The circumference is then multiplied by the pipe length to find the material in one piece. The result is multiplied by the quantity to determine the total amount of material needed, then divided by 144 to convert the answer to square feet. The final quantity is carried to the next square foot by adding one and using the INTEGER function to select only the whole number to the left of the decimal place.

Place your cursor on C7 and type:

@INT(	selects the value to the left of the decimal point
C4	coordinate containing diameter
*	multiplies
@PI	3.1415926536 (multiplier)
*	multiplies
C3	coordinate containing pipe length
*	multiplies
C2	coordinate containing quantity
/	divides
144)	value used to convert to sq. ft.
+	adds
1	value
RETURN	enters the formula

Formula five, to the immediate right of Manufacture time, calculates the manufacturing time to produce the number of pipes indicated, by dividing the square feet of material by the number of square feet per hour the selected machine will process. The LOOKUP function is used to find the production rate of the selected machine in the Machine Production Rate Table. To round out the result to the next whole hour, one is added to the answer and the INTEGER function is used to select only the whole number to the left of the decimal point.

Place your cursor on C8 and type:

@INT(	selects the value to the left of the decimal point
C7	coordinate containing total sq. ft. needed
/	divides
@VLOOKUP(	starts LOOKUP function
C6,	coordinate containing value to be looked up
TABLE4,	name of Range
2))	second offset
+	adds
1	number used to round out to next whole hour
RETURN	executes the command

Formula six, to the immediate right of Manufacturing Cost, uses the LOOKUP function to select the hourly cost rate of the machine being used from the Machine Hourly Cost Table. It then multiplies that rate times the hours listed for Manufacturing Time to obtain the Manufacturing Cost.

Place your cursor on C9 and type:

@VLOOKUP(	starts LOOKUP function
C6,	coordinate containing value to be looked up
TABLE4,	name of Range
1)	first offset
*	multiplies
C8	coordinate containing manufacturing time
RETURN	enters the formula

To format in dollars and cents, leave your cursor on C9 and type:

/R	starts RANGE command

F	selects Format option
C	selects Currency option and displays # of decimal places: 2
RETURN	displays range to format C9..C9
RETURN	executes the command

Formula seven, to the immediate right of Material Cost, calculates the Material Cost. The LOOKUP function is first used to determine the material purchase cost from the Mat'l Grade Cost/Sq Ft table. A second LOOKUP function is used to determine the percentage rate of the pricing markup from the percent of Cost Markup table. The resulting values from these two LOOKUP functions are multiplied and the answer multiplied by the total sq. ft. needed value to obtain the Material Cost.

Place your cursor on C10 and type:

@VLOOKUP(	starts LOOKUP function
C1,	coordinate containing value to be looked up
TABLE6,	name of Range
1)	first offset
*	multiplies
@VLOOKUP(	starts LOOKUP function
C7,	coordinate containing value to be looked up
TABLE5,	name of Range
1)	first offset
*	multiplies
C7	coordinate containing total sq. ft. needed
RETURN	enters the formula

To format in dollars and cents, leave your cursor on C10 and type:

/R	starts RANGE command
F	selects Format option

C	selects Currency option and displays # of decimal places: 2
RETURN	displays Range to format C10..C10
RETURN	executes the command

Formula eight, to the immediate right of Total Job Cost, will add the total of the values listed for Manufacturing Cost and Material Cost, and display the answer on the Total Job Cost line.

Place your cursor on C12 and type:

@SUM(	adds values in list
C9	first coordinate of column to add
.	ellipsis—indicates from-to
C11)	last coordinate of column to add
RETURN	enters the formula

To format in dollars and cents, leave your cursor on C12 and type:

/R	starts RANGE command
F	selects Format option
C	selects Currency option and displays # of decimal places: 2
RETURN	displays Range to format C12..C12
RETURN	executes the command

Your estimating sheet is now complete. To observe its operations, enter your measurement and material grade values on the appropriate lines at the top of the page (Figure 3).

SAVING

You may wish to save your entire worksheet. To do this leave your cursor on any location and type:

| /F | starts FILE command |
| S | selects SAVE option |

Type in name of file. Do not leave spaces between words.

| RETURN | executes the command |

```
        A         B        C        D        E        F        G        H        I

 1 Material Grade:        300
 2 Quantity:              150
 3 Length,Feet:            30
 4 Diameter, Inch           4
 5
 6 Machine To Use:          6
 7 Total SqFt Needed:     393
 8 Manufacture Time        16
 9 Manufacturing Cost   $296.80
10 Material Cost:       4642.3125
11                      ============
12 Total Job Cost       $4,939.11
13
14 Table1                        Table2                    Table3
15 ------------------            Machine To Use            Machine To Use
16      1        4               Diameter Machine #        Length   Machine #
17      2        6               ------------------        ------------------
18                                    1        1                0        4
19                                    2        2               20        5
20                                    3        3               25        6
21                                    4        4
22                                    5        7
23
24 Table4                        Table5                    Table6
25 Hrly Machine Cost             Markup Percentage         Mat'l Grade Cost
26 & Production Rate             Quantity Percent          Material Cost/SqFt
27 Machine # Price/Hr SqFt/Hr    ------------------        ------------------
28 -----------------------------       0      2.5              100     5.75
29      1     25.55      36           100      2.25            150     4.85
30      2     30.55      45           300      1.75            200     3.79
31      3     20.25      50           500      1.5             250     5.55
32      4     45.55      60          1000      1.25            300     6.75
33      5     56.85      45
34      6     18.55      25
35      7    125.55      75
```

Figure 3

PRINTING

To print out all or a portion of your worksheet, use the following directions, which are given for the Epson printer (compressed font).

Place your cursor on A1 and type:

/P	starts PRINT command
P	displays options
O	selects Options option
S	selects Setup option and displays Enter Setup String
\015	sets an Epson printer to compressed font
RETURN	accepts setup and displays options
M	selects Margin option
R	selects Right option
230	characters per line
RETURN	displays options
Q	selects Quit option and returns to main print menu
R	displays Range to print from
.	ellipsis—indicates from-to

Move cursor, with arrow keys, to last coordinate in area you wish to print. The screen will reverse to indicate the area being printed.

RETURN	executes the command
G	selects Go option and prints

To exit out of PRINT command, type:

Q	selects Quit option and exits out of PRINT command

EXERCISE FIVE

CHECKBOOK LEDGER

DESCRIPTION

The Lotus 1-2-3 program allows you to do ledger postings and accumulate the postings, and add or subtract the resulting value from a balance figure, and then update and maintain year-to-date totals.

To demonstrate these techniques, a checkbook worksheet has been set up which allows us to make deposits and payments entries, which allows you to keep a running total of the balance. Once a month the checkbook is updated, allowing you to keep year-to-date information. 1-2-3's powerful Keyboard Macros is used to allow the updating process to be accomplished with a single keystroke.

OPERATIONS PERFORMED

Setting Up The Worksheet Format

Entering Mathematical Formulas

Protecting Mathematical Formula Entries

Posting Entries

Naming Groups of Coordinates

Monthly Updating

Updating Using Keyboard Macros

Saving

Printing

FUNCTIONS USED

SUM
IF

COMMANDS USED

COPY	copies formulas
FILE	saves values
FILE	moves
FILE	saves worksheet
PRINT	prints worksheet
RANGE	formats in integer
RANGE	erases
RANGE	protects formulas
RANGE	names coordinates
RANGE	centers labels
REPEAT	repeats dashed lines
WORKSHEET	adjusts column width
WORKSHEET	formats in 2 decimal places

SETTING UP THE WORKSHEET FORMAT

Using the following directions, set up and label the exercise format on your worksheet, copying Figure 1 exactly as it is illustrated, retaining exact row and column locations of all information.

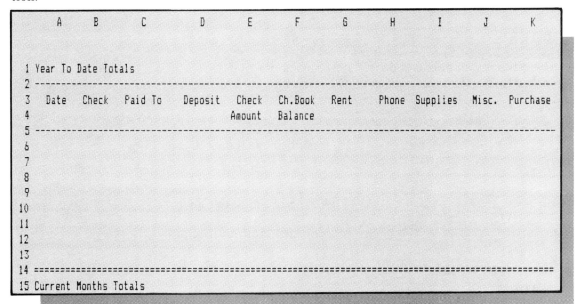

Figure 1

NOTE

Enter your column headings. After entering your column headings, you will center them in the columns by using the Center option.

Place your cursor on A3 and type:

/R	starts RANGE command
L	selects Label-Prefix option
C	selects Center option and displays Range of labels A3..A3

Move your cursor to K4. Notice the screen is reversing to show you which coordinates are to be formatted.

RETURN	executes the command

To enter dashed lines on your worksheet, place your cursor on the left-most column of the row where you want the line (A2 in this example.)

Type:

\	starts REPEAT command
—	label to be repeated
RETURN	executes the command

The column your cursor is on will now have a line of dashes across its width. To extend the dashed line in the same row across the remaining columns, leave your cursor where it is and type:

/C	starts COPY command and displays Range to copy from
RETURN	displays Range to copy to
B2	first coordinate to copy to
•	ellipsis—indicates from-to
K2	last coordinate to copy to
RETURN	executes the command

The dashed line will now appear extended across the columns you have indicated by your coordinates. To enter a double-dashed line on the worksheet, repeat the operations above, using the symbol = as your label to be repeated.

The 1-2-3 worksheet format contains columns nine spaces wide when it is first entered into the computer. Individual columns or all of the columns on the worksheet may be expanded to contain more spaces, or compressed to contain fewer spaces, with a command function. In this exercise, you will expand the width of all columns, and then reduce column B.

First expand the width of all the columns. Type:

/W	starts WORKSHEET command
G	selects Global option
C	selects Column-Width option
12	number of spaces in column
RETURN	executes the command

To reduce the width of column B, place your cursor on column B and type:

/W   starts WORKSHEET command

C   selects Column-Width option

S   selects Set option and displays
                            column width

6   number of spaces in column

RETURN   executes the command

To format all value locations on your worksheet to display dollars and cents, type:

/W   starts WORKSHEET command

G   selects Global option

F   selects Format option

F   selects Fixed option and displays
                            number of decimal places: 2

RETURN   executes the command

Because you will be listing check numbers in column B, you do not want the coordinates in that column to read values in dollars and cents. You will now change the format for that column of coordinates to read whole numbers using the INTEGER function.

To format column B to read in whole numbers, place your cursor on B6 and type:

/R   starts RANGE command

F   selects Format option

F   selects Fixed format

0   number of decimal places

RETURN   displays Range to format: B6..B6

Move your cursor to B13 with arrow keys. Notice the screen is reversing to show you which coordinates are to be formatted.

RETURN   executes the command

ENTERING MATHEMATICAL FORMULAS

You will now begin entering mathematical formulas that will establish the relationships between column and row positions. The formulas and their locations are illustrated in Figure 2.

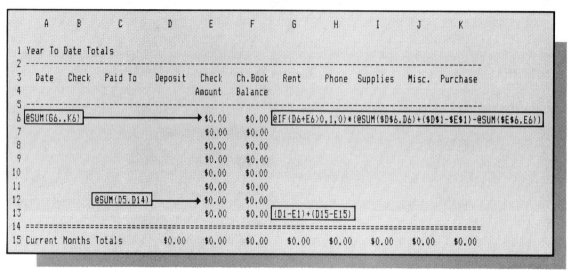

Figure 2

Formula one, in the Check Amount column, will add the total of the postings from the Rent column across to the Purchase column on each row, and display the result in the Check Amount column.

Place your cursor on E6 and type:

@SUM(	adds values in the following list
G6	first coordinate of row to add
.	ellipsis—indicates from-to
K6)	last coordinate of row to add
RETURN	enters the formula

Formula two, in the Ch. Book Balance column, determines the CH. BOOK BALANCE. The first half of calculation in the formula uses the IF function which selects the value one if an amount is greater than zero in the Deposit or Check Amount column. If the two columns equal zero or less than zero, a zero is selected. The result of this calculation is used to enter a zero in a row where no entries have yet been made. The second half of the formula adds the Deposit listings to the Year To Date Deposits minus the Year To Date check amounts, and subtracts the check amount listed on the row. The resulting value is multiplied by a one if a transaction has taken place, and displays the check book balance. A zero is displayed if no transaction has taken place.

_____ **NOTE** _____

1-2-3 is designed to do one of two things with coordinates when they are copied. The coordinates are either relative to their new location or they remain absolute, which means they remain the same.

A coordinate address is relative unless it is converted to an absolute by having a dollar sign ($) preceding the column designation and/or row designation, i.e. ($G$8).

A quick way to make a coordinate absolute is by placing your cursor on that coordinate and pressing the F4 key, which will place the dollar as shown automatically.

Place your cursor on F6 and type:

@IF(	if the first expression is true, uses the second expression; if not, uses expression three
D6 + E6 > 0	first expression-is the sum of the Check Amount and Ch. Book Balance entries greater than zero?
,	comma—separates expressions in the formula
1	second expression—will be selected if the first expression is true
,	comma—separates expressions in the formula
0	third expression—will be selected if the first expression is not true
)	parenthesis-separates calculations in the formula
*	multiplies
(	parenthesis—separates calculations in the formula
@SUM(	adds values in the following list

$D$6	value to be added Note: $ converts coordinate to an absolute address
.	ellipsis—indicates from-to
D6)	value to be added
+	adds
($D$1—$E$1)	YTD deposit minus YTD check amount Note: $ converts coordinate to an absolute address
—	subtracts
@SUM(	adds values in the following list
$E$6	value to be added Note: $ converts coordinate to an absolute address
.	ellipsis—indicates from-to
E6	value to be added
))	parenthesis—closes sum function
RETURN	enters the formula

Now copy the formulas in the Check Amount and Ch. Book Balance columns down into the rows in each column down to the double-dashed line, using the COPY command.

To begin your COPY operation, leave your cursor on any location and type:

/C	starts COPY command and displays Range to copy from
E6	first coordinate to copy from
.	ellipsis—indicates from-to
F6	last coordinate to copy from
RETURN	displays range to copy to
E7	first coordinate to copy to
.	ellipsis—indicates from-to

| E13 | last coordinate to copy to |
| RETURN | executes the command |

Formula three, in the Current Months Total, Deposit, column, adds current months total and deposit.

Place your cursor on D15 and type:

@SUM(	adds values in the following list
D5	first coordinate of column to add
•	ellipsis—indicates from-to
D14)	last cell of column to add
RETURN	enters the formula

Now copy the formula you have just entered across under the remaining column to the right on your worksheet, using the COPY command.

Leave your cursor on D15 and type:

/C	starts COPY command and displays Range to copy from
RETURN	displays Range to copy to
E15	first coordinate to copy to
•	ellipsis—indicates from-to
K15	last coordinate to copy to
RETURN	executes the command

Formula four, in the Check Book Balance column, in the Current Months Total row, uses a special formula to obtain the total on its CURRENT MONTH TOTALS line. For this reason, you will now replace the formula in that location with a new formula.

To enter formula four:

Place your cursor on F15 and type:

(D1—E1)	Year To Date Deposit minus Year To Date check amounts
+	adds
(D15—E15)	Current Months deposits minus Current Months check amounts
RETURN	enters the formula

PROTECTING MATHEMATICAL FORMULA ENTRIES

To protect our formulas on our checkbook so that they are not erased accidentally by either erasing the formulas or typing into their coordinate locations by mistake, we will utilize the 1-2-3 ability to protect these coordinates.

To do this, you will first turn on the PROTECT option under the WORKSHEET commands, and then you will go back and unprotect only the coordinates which you will want to be able to type into. To protect all coordinates, type:

/W	starts WORKSHEET command
G	selects Global option
P	selects Protection option
E	selects Enable option

The next operation is to unprotect only the coordinates you wish to type into, Date through Deposit columns.

Place your cursor on A6 and type:

/R	starts RANGE command
U	selects Unprotect option

Move your cursor to D13 with your arrow keys. Screen will reverse to display coordinates being unprotected.

RETURN	executes the command

Next set of columns to unprotect are Rent through Purchases.

Place your cursor on G6 and type:

/R	starts RANGE command
U	selects Unprotect option

Move your cursor to K13 with your arrow keys. Screen will reverse to display coordinates being unprotected.

RETURN	executes the command

The last coordinate to unprotect will be Check Book Balance in the Year To Date row.

Place your cursor on F1 and type:

/R	starts RANGE command
U	selects Unprotect option
RETURN	executes the command

POSTING ENTRIES

You may now begin posting entries in your checkbook worksheet to observe its operation. Sample entries are shown in Figure 3. You may use them, if you wish, to check the operation of your worksheet against the illustration.

————————————— **NOTE** —————————————

Post check amounts in disbursements columns: Rent, Phone, Supplies, Misc. and Purchase.

	A	B	C	D	E	F	G	H	I	J	K
1	Year To Date Totals										
2	--										
3	Date	Check	Paid To	Deposit	Check	Ch.Book	Rent	Phone	Supplies	Misc.	Purchase
4					Amount	Balance					
5	--										
6	Feb 18			1000.00	0.00	1000.00					
7	Feb 20	100	Tiffany Co		120.00	880.00					120.00
8	Feb 20	101	RK Williams		100.00	780.00			100.00		
9	Feb 21	102	Bell Phone		50.00	730.00		50.00			
10	Feb 28	103	Noll Bldg		550.00	180.00	500.00			50.00	
11					0.00	0.00					
12					0.00	0.00					
13					0.00	0.00					
14	==										
15	Current Months Totals			1000.00	820.00	180.00	500.00	50.00	100.00	50.00	120.00

Figure 3

To make a deposit entry, type in the deposit amount. To make a check value entry, place your cursor on the desired space in the appropriate expense column. Following any value entry, type RETURN to enter the value into the coordinate.

NAMING GROUPS OF COORDINATES

Before updating, we will name several parts of the worksheet to make the updating procedure go quickly and easily.

The first group of coordinates to be named will be Date through Deposit, between the single and double dashed lines: DATE.

The second group of coordinates to be named will be Rent through Purchases, between the single and double dashed lines: CHECKS.

The third group of coordinates to be named will be Current Months Totals: MTD.

To name the first group of coordinates, place your cursor on A6 and type:

/R	starts RANGE command
N	selects Name option
C	selects Create option
DATE	name
RETURN	displays Enter Range: A6..A6

Move your cursor to D13, with the arrow keys. The screen will reverse to show you which coordinate locations are being named.

RETURN	executes the command

To name the second group of coordinates, place your cursor on G6 and type:

/R	starts RANGE command
N	selects Name option
C	selects Create option

| CHECKS | name of range |
| RETURN | displays Enter Range: G6..G6 |

Move your cursor to K13, with the arrow keys. The screen will reverse to show you which coordinate locations are being named.

| RETURN | executes the command |

To name the third group of coordinates, place your cursor on D15 and type:

/R	starts RANGE command
N	selects Name option
C	selects Create option
MTD	name of range
RETURN	displays Enter Range: D15..D15

Move your cursor to K15, with the arrow keys. The screen will reverse to show you which coordinate locations are being named.

| RETURN | executes the command |

MONTHLY UPDATING

Now that the coordinates are named, we will want to first save the MTD out to disk, and then we will move it back onto the worksheet onto the YTD Totals row.

With your cursor on any location, type:

/F	starts FILE command
X	selects Xtract option
V	selects Value option which saves only the values
MTD	filename
RETURN	displays Range
MTD	name of columns
RETURN	executes the command

To move the MTD back onto the worksheet onto the Year To Date Totals row, which will add the MTD total to the YTD, making new YTD totals,

Place your cursor on D1 and type:

/F	starts FILE command
C	selects Combine option
A	selects Add option
E	selects Entire File option
MTD	filename
RETURN	executes the command

The next operation to perform is to erase the information in Date through Deposit columns. Type:

/R	starts RANGE command
E	selects Erase option and displays range to erase
DATE	name of Range
RETURN	executes the command

The next operation to perform is to erase the information in Rent through Purchase columns. Type:

/R	starts RANGE command
E	selects Erase option and displays range to erase
CHECKS	name of Range
RETURN	executes the command

The final operation is to erase the YTD Total in the Ch. Book Balance column. It must first be unprotected.

Place your cursor on F1 and type:

/R	starts RANGE command
U	selects Unprotect option
RETURN	executes the command
/R	starts RANGE command
E	selects Erase option
RETURN	executes the command

Your worksheet should look like Figure 4, when complete.

	A	B	C	D	E	F	G	H	I	J	K
1	Year To Date Totals			1000.00	820.00		500.00	50.00	100.00	50.00	120.00
2	--
3	Date	Check	Paid To	Deposit	Check	Ch.Book	Rent	Phone	Supplies	Misc.	Purchase
4					Amount	Balance					
5	--
6					0.00	0.00					
7					0.00	0.00					
8					0.00	0.00					
9					0.00	0.00					
10					0.00	0.00					
11					0.00	0.00					
12					0.00	0.00					
13					0.00	0.00					
14	==
15	Current Months Totals			0.00	0.00	180.00	0.00	0.00	0.00	0.00	0.00

Figure 4

Now make new entries into your worksheet.

UPDATING WITH KEYBOARD MACROS

1-2-3 has an extremely powerful feature which is called Keyboard Macros, which allows you to set up a string of keystroke information in a small file, enabling you to perform an operation, such as the MONTHLY updating we just did, with a single keystroke.

To set up the Keyboard Macros, you will first need to enter the keystroke information into a coordinate or a group of adjacent coordinates in a column.

Next you will need to name the coordinate or group of coordinates which contain the keystroke information, using a backslash followed by any single character from A to Z. Example: \A.

First we will enter the Keystroke Macros file.

_____ **NOTE** _____

An apostrophe (') is entered at the beginning of each line to prepare coordinates for label information.

The ˉ represents a RETURN.

We have put an r after the filename RETURN because the computer asks if you want to Replace or Cancel a file which already exists on the disk. The R represents the Replace.

{goto} moves cursor to the coordinate following it.

_____

First unprotect A18 through A23.

Place your cursor on A18 and type:

/R   starts RANGE command

U   selects Unprotect option

Move your cursor to A23 with arrow keys. Screen will reverse to show which coordinate locations are being unprotected.

RETURN   executes the command

Now enter the Keyboard Macros file.

Place your cursor on A18 and type:

› /fxvMTD^MTD^r
› {goto}D1^/fcaeMTD^
› /reDATE^
› /reCHECKS^
› {goto}F1^/ru^
› /re^

Second operation will be to name the coordinates containing the Keyboard Macros.

	A	B	C	D	E	F	G	H	I	J	K
1	Year To Date Totals			1000.00	820.00		500.00	50.00	100.00	50.00	120.00
2	--
3	Date	Check	Paid To	Deposit	Check	Ch.Book	Rent	Phone	Supplies	Misc.	Purchase
4					Amount	Balance					
5	--
6	March 1	302	Adams Co	1000.00	500.00	680.00	500.00				
7	March 3	303	Roberts Co	800.00	90.00	1390.00					
8	March 6	304	Sitton Co		50.00	1340.00			90.00		
9	March 21	305	Gold Co		700.00	640.00			50.00		
10	March 22	306	Isaacson Co		180.00	460.00				700.00	
11					0.00	0.00					180.00
12					0.00	0.00					
13					0.00	0.00					
14	==
15	Current Months Totals			1800.00	1520.00	460.00	500.00	0.00	140.00	700.00	180.00
16											
17											
18	/fxvMTD^MTD^r
19	{goto}D1^/fcaeMTD^
20	/reDATE^
21	/reCHECKS^
22	{goto}F1^/ru^
23	/re^

Figure 5

Place your cursor on A18 and type:

/R	starts RANGE command
N	selects Name option
C	selects Create option
\A	name of coordinate
RETURN	displays Range: A18..A18

Move your cursor to A23 with arrow keys. Screen will reverse to display area being named.

| RETURN | executes the command |

Your worksheet should look like Figure 5.

Now that the keyboard macros file is named, and your new entries have been made, to demonstrate its use, and to execute the macros,

Hold the Alt key down and press A.

Your worksheet should look like Figure 6.

	A	B	C	D	E	F	G	H	I	J	K
1	Year To Date Totals			2800.00	2340.00		1000.00	50.00	240.00	750.00	300.00
2	---
3	Date	Check	Paid To	Deposit	Check	Ch.Book	Rent	Phone	Supplies	Misc.	Purchase
4					Amount	Balance
5	---
6					0.00	0.00
7					0.00	0.00
8					0.00	0.00
9					0.00	0.00
10					0.00	0.00
11					0.00	0.00
12					0.00	0.00
13					0.00	0.00
14	===
15	Current Months Totals			0.00	0.00	460.00	0.00	0.00	0.00	0.00	0.00
16	
17	
18	/fxvMTD^MTD^r
19	{goto}D1^/fcaeMTD^
20	/reDATE^
21	/reCHECKS^
22	{goto}F1^/ru^
23	/re^

Figure 6

SAVING

You may wish to save your entire worksheet. To do this leave your cursor on any location and type:

/F	starts FILE command
S	selects SAVE option

Type in name of file. Do not leave spaces between words.

RETURN	executes the command

PRINTING

To print out all or a portion of your worksheet, following the following directions, which are given for the Epson printer (compressed font).

Place your cursor on A1 and type:

/P	starts PRINT command
P	displays options
O	selects Options option
S	selects Setup option and displays Enter Setup String
\015	sets an Epson printer to compressed font
RETURN	accepts setup and displays options
M	selects Margin option
R	selects Right option
230	characters per line
RETURN	displays options
Q	selects Quit option and returns to main print menu
R	displays Range to print from
.	ellipsis—indicates from-to

Move cursor, with arrow keys, to last coordinate in area you wish to print. The screen will reverse to indicates the area being printed.

RETURN   executes the command

G   selects Go option and prints

To exit out of PRINT command, type:

Q   selects Quit option and exits
                                out of PRINT command

EXERCISE SIX

INVOICING FROM INVENTORY

DESCRIPTION

The Lotus 1-2-3 program selects values from reference tables and uses those values in problem solving. The exercise also illustrates the calculation of a value from predetermined limits on a graduated scale, and changing a value within a set to include application of discount, sales tax, or some other modifying factor.

To demonstrate 1-2-3's ability, an Invoicing from Inventory worksheet is used. Inventory numerical identification, description and quantity are entered on lines in the invoice. The invoice format then automatically calculates the single price for each item and the total for the quantity ordered, adds the invoice total, applies a discount and sales tax factor and displays a grand total. A sales commission is calculated from the invoice net value and displayed in a salesperson commission report.

OPERATIONS PERFORMED

Setting Up The Format

Entering Mathematical Formulas

Saving

Printing

FUNCTIONS USED

LOOKUP
MAX
MIN
SUM

COMMANDS USED

COPY	copies formulas
FILE	saves worksheet
PRINT	prints worksheet
RANGE	formats in 2 decimal places
RANGE	centers labels
REPEAT	repeats dashed lines
WORKSHEET	adjusts column width

SETTING UP THE WORKSHEET FORMAT

To set up your beginning format, use the following directions, copying Figure 1 exactly as it is illustrated, retaining exact row and column locations of all information.

The 1-2-3 worksheet format contains columns nine spaces wide when it is first entered into the computer. Column width may be expanded using the following commands. In this exercise, you will use columns with 14 spaces.

To widen all your columns, type:

/W	starts WORKSHEET command
G	selects Global option
C	selects Column-Width option
14	number of spaces in column
RETURN	executes the command

Enter your column headings. Next you will center them in the columns by using the Center option.

Place your cursor on A10 and type:

/R	starts RANGE command
L	selects Label-Prefix option
C	selects Center option and displays Range of labels A10-A10

Move your cursor to E10. Notice the screen is reversing to show you what coordinates are to be centered.

RETURN	executes the command

To enter dashed lines on your worksheet, place your cursor on the left-most column of the row where you want the line to begin (A11 in this example.)

Type:

\	starts REPEAT command
—	label to be repeated
RETURN	executes the command

```
         A           B          C           D           E         F          G          H

 1 Invoice Number
 2
 3 Customer Name
 4    Address:
 5       City:
 6      State:                 Zip Code:
 7
 8 Salesperson No                         Date:
 9
10   Quantity      Item No.   Description   Unit Cost    Total Cost
11 -----------------------------------------------------------------------
12
13
14
15
16
17
18
19
20 =======================================================================
21                                          Freight:
22                                         Sub Total:
23                                          Discount:
24                                               Net:
25                                         Sales Tax:
26                                                     ==============
27                                       Grand Total:
28
29 Salesperson Commission Rpt.
30 ---------------------------
31 Salesperson No
32 Invoice Number
33    Commission
34
35 ---------------------------      ---------------------------      ---------------------------
36 Pricing Table                    Pricing Table                        Discount Table
37 For Paper Prod       Price       For Glassware        Price        Amount       Percent
38 ---------------------------      ---------------------------      ---------------------------
39        0             0                  0             0                  0             0
40      100             0.55             200             0.36             100            10
41      125             0.25             225             0.59             200            12
42      128             1.33             226             1.23             300            15
43      129             0.63             230             0.89             500            18
44      130             0.75             255             3.25
45      131             1.58             275             1.45
46      132             2.36             276             0.65
47      133             0                 280             0
```

Figure 1

The column your cursor is on will now have a line of dashes across its width. To extend the dashed line in the same row across the remaining columns, leave your cursor where it is and type:

/C	starts COPY command and displays Range to copy from
RETURN	displays Range to copy to
B11	first coordinate to copy to
.	ellipsis—indicates from-to
E11	last coordinate to copy to
RETURN	executes the command

The dashed line will now appear extended across the columns you have indicated by your coordinates. To enter a double-dashed line on the worksheet, repeat the operations above, using the symbol = as your label to be repeated.

ENTERING MATHEMATICAL FORMULAS

You will now begin entering mathematical formulas that will establish the relationships between column and row positions. The formulas and their locations are illustrated in Figure 2.

Formula one will search two reference tables for the inventory number (Item No.) listed on the invoice, pick up the price listed in the table to the right of that number and enter it in the Unit Cost column on the invoice. The tables in this exercise have been purposely set up to demonstrate multi-table search capability. Because of the unique features contained in this operation, an extensive description of the logic has been provided.

The LOOKUP function is used to control selection of the appropriate table and to locate the desired value in the selected table. Two LOOKUP functions are used in this example, to search for the desired value in each of two tables.

When a LOOKUP function fails to detect a value as large as that it has been asked to search for, it will select the largest value in the table and enter the number to the right of it into the formula. To accommodate the LOOKUP search from the end of one column to the beginning of the next, zero has been listed to the right of the last number in each column. If the LOOKUP number is larger than the last number in a column, it will pick up and enter the value opposite the last number in the formula.

If the LOOKUP value is smaller than the first whole number in a table, it will display ERROR. In this exercise, zero has been listed in the first position of each table to enable the LOOKUP

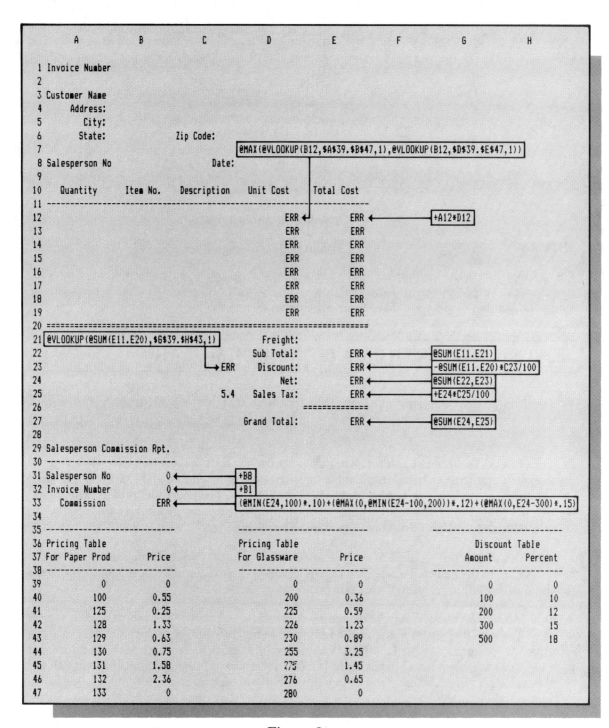

```
              A            B            C            D            E            F            G            H

 1 Invoice Number
 2
 3 Customer Name
 4     Address:
 5        City:
 6       State:                      Zip Code:
 7                                              @MAX(@VLOOKUP(B12,$A$39.$B$47,1),@VLOOKUP(B12,$D$39.$E$47,1))
 8 Salesperson No                    Date:
 9
10    Quantity     Item No.    Description    Unit Cost    Total Cost
11 ------------------------------------------------------------------
12                                              ERR          ERR           +A12*D12
13                                              ERR          ERR
14                                              ERR          ERR
15                                              ERR          ERR
16                                              ERR          ERR
17                                              ERR          ERR
18                                              ERR          ERR
19                                              ERR          ERR
20 ================================================================
21 @VLOOKUP(@SUM(E11.E20),$G$39.$H$43,1)        Freight:
22                                     Sub Total:   ERR           @SUM(E11.E21)
23                             ERR     Discount:    ERR           -@SUM(E11.E20)*C23/100
24                                          Net:    ERR           @SUM(E22,E23)
25                             5.4     Sales Tax:   ERR           +E24*C25/100
26                                              ===============
27                                  Grand Total:    ERR           @SUM(E24,E25)
28
29 Salesperson Commission Rpt.
30 ---------------------------
31 Salesperson No          0             +B8
32 Invoice Number          0             +B1
33    Commission         ERR             (@MIN(E24,100)*.10)+(@MAX(0,@MIN(E24-100,200))*.12)+(@MAX(0,E24-300)*.15)
34
35 ---------------           ---------------------        ---------------------------
36 Pricing Table            Pricing Table                    Discount Table
37 For Paper Prod   Price   For Glassware    Price        Amount        Percent
38 ---------------          ---------------------        ---------------------------
39        0          0             0           0             0             0
40      100         0.55          200         0.36         100            10
41      125         0.25          225         0.59         200            12
42      128         1.33          226         1.23         300            15
43      129         0.63          230         0.89         500            18
44      130         0.75          255         3.25
45      131         1.58          275         1.45
46      132         2.36          276         0.65
47      133          0            280          0
```

Figure 2

function to pick up and use the number to the right of that first listing when the first whole number is less than the LOOKUP number. The value 0 is listed to the right of these first position entries to supply that value to the formula.

In the table containing the LOOKUP value, the LOOKUP function will pick up and enter the number to the right of that value into the formula. In the table not containing the LOOKUP value, the LOOKUP function will pick up and list zero into the formula. The formula is constructed to select the largest value selected by the LOOKUP functions contained within it.

--- **NOTE** ---

All tables in this exercise are in a vertical format which means the tables are in column format. the left-most column of the table is considered the labels of the table, and the adjacent columns to the right contain the values. The second column of the table is considered as the first offset. The third column of the table is considered the second offset, and etc. LOOKUP function being used will be indicated by @VLOOKUP.

(If the tables were in a horizontal format, or row format, the top-most row would be the labels, and the rows beneath it would be the values, the second row being the first offset, etc. The LOOKUP function being used would be indicated by @HLOOKUP.)

--- **NOTE** ---

1-2-3 is designed to do one of two things with coordinates when they are copied. The coordinates are either relative to their new location or they remain absolute, which means they remain the same.

A coordinate address is relative unless it is converted to an absolute by having a dollar sign ($) preceding the column designation and/or row designation, i.e. (GB).

A quick way to make a coordinate absolute is by placing your cursor on that coordinate and pressing the F4 key, which will place the dollar as shown automatically.

To enter formula one,

Place your cursor on D12 and type:

@MAX(	selects the maximum value of the following list
@VLOOKUP(	starts LOOKUP function

B12,	coordinate containing value to look up
$A$39.$B$47,	Table range Note: $ converts coordinate to an absolute address
1),	first offset
@VLOOKUP(	starts LOOKUP function
B12,	coordinate containing value to look up
$D$39.$E$47,	Table range Note: $ converts coordinate to an absolute address
1))	first offset
RETURN	enters the formula

To format to display in 2 decimal places,

Leave your cursor on D12 and type:

/R	starts RANGE command
F	selects Format option
F	selects Fixed option and displays number of decimal places: 2
RETURN	displays Range to format D12..D12
RETURN	executes the command

Formula two multiplies the Unit Cost by Quantity and displays it in the Total Cost column in dollars and cents format.

Place your cursor on E12 and type:

+A12	picks up coordinate containing value from Quantity column
*	multiplies
D12	picks up coordinate containing value from Unit Cost column
RETURN	enters the formula

To format to display in 2 decimal places,

Leave your cursor on E12 and type:

/R	starts RANGE command
F	selects Format option
F	selects Fixed option and displays number of decimal places: 2
RETURN	displays Range to format E12..E12
RETURN	executes the command

Your next operation is to copy the formulas just entered at the top of each column into each row in the respective columns.

Leave your cursor on any location and type:

/C	starts COPY command and displays Range to copy from
D12	first cell to copy from
.	ellipsis—indicates from-to
E12	last cell to copy from
RETURN	displays range to copy to
D13	first cell to copy to
.	ellipsis—indicates from-to
D19	last cell to copy to
RETURN	executes the command

Formula three will add the sum of the values in the Total Cost column above the double-dashed line and the Freight value. The answer will be displayed as Sub Total, in dollars and cents format.

Place your cursor on E22 and type:

@SUM(	adds values in the list
E11	first coordinate of column to add
.	ellipsis—indicates from-to

E21)	last coordinate of column to add
RETURN	enters the formula

To format to display in 2 decimal places,

Place your cursor on E22 and type:

/R	starts RANGE command
F	selects Format option
F	selects Fixed option and displays number of decimal places: 2
RETURN	displays Range to format E22..E22
RETURN	executes the command

Formula four enters a LOOKUP function that will use the sum of Total Cost column to select an appropriate discount rate from the Discount Table (containing a graduated set of values and display it to the left of Discount.)

─────────────────────── **NOTE** ───────────────────────

1-2-3 is designed to do one of two things with coordinates when they are copied. The coordinates are either relative to their new location or they remain absolute, which means they remain the same.

A coordinate address is relative unless it is converted to an absolute by having a dollar sign ($) preceding the column designation and/or row designation, i.e. ($G$8).

A quick way to make a coordinate absolute is by placing your cursor on that coordinate and pressing the F4 key, which will place the dollar as shown automatically.

───

Place your cursor on C23 and type:

@VLOOKUP(	starts LOOKUP function
@SUM(	adds values in the list
E11	first coordinate of column to add
•	ellipsis—indicates from-to
E20)	last coordinate of column to add
,	comma—separates LOOKUP value from discount table coordinates

$G$39.$H$43,	Table range Note: $ converts coordinate to an absolute address
1)	first offset
RETURN	enters the formula

Formula five will add the sum of the Total Cost column above the double-dashed line, multiply the result by the discount rate and divide the answer by 100 to arrive at a percentage value. the resulting discount allowance will be displayed on the Discount line in dollars and cents as a negative value.

Place your cursor on E23 and type:

—@SUM(	adds values in the list and displays the result as a negative value
E11	first coordinate of column to add
•	ellipsis—indicates from-to
E20)	last coordinate of column to add
*	multiplies
C23	coordinate containing value
/	divides
100	value
RETURN	enters the formula

To format to display in 2 decimal places,

Place your cursor on E23 and type:

/R	starts RANGE command
F	selects Format option
F	selects Fixed option and displays number of decimal places: 2
RETURN	displays Range to format E23..E23
RETURN	executes the command

Formula six uses the SUM function to calculate the value of the Sub Total less Discount. The result will be displayed on the Net line in dollars and cents format.

Place your cursor on E24 and type:

@SUM(	adds values in the list
E22	coordinate containing value
,	comma—separates values in the list
E23)	coordinate containing value
RETURN	enters the formula

To format to display in 2 decimal places,

Leave your cursor on E24 and type:

/R	starts RANGE command
F	selects Format option
F	selects Fixed option and displays number of decimal places: 2
RETURN	displays Range to format E24..E24
RETURN	executes the command

The next operation enters the sales tax.

Place your cursor on C25 and type:

5.4	sales tax rate used in the example
RETURN	enters the value

Formula seven determines sales tax on the net invoiced amount. Multiply the Net value times that rate and divide the result by 100 to arrive at a percentage value. The tax amount will then be displayed on the Sales Tax line in dollars and cents format.

Place your cursor on E25 and type:

+E24	coordinate containing value to be multiplied by the sales tax rate
*	multiplies
C25	coordinate containing the sales tax rate value

/	divides
100	value
RETURN	enters the formula

To format to display in 2 decimal places,

Leave your cursor on E25 and type:

/R	starts RANGE command
F	selects Format option
F	selects Fixed option and displays number of decimal places: 2
RETURN	displays Range to format E25..E25
RETURN	executes the command

Formula eight adds the Net and the Sales Tax values. The result will display on the Grand Total line in dollars and cents format.

Place your cursor on E27 and type:

@SUM(	adds values in the list
E24	coordinate containing value
,	comma—separates values in the list
E25)	coordinate containing value
RETURN	enters the formula

To format to display in currency,

Leave your cursor on E27 and type:

/R	starts RANGE command
F	selects Format option
C	selects Currency option and displays # of decimal places: 2
RETURN	displays Range to format E27..E27
RETURN	executes the command

Formulas nine, ten and eleven will record the invoice and salesman's numbers on the Salesperson Commission Rpt., and calculate the salesperson's commission. The commission will be determined by comparing the invoice Net value against a set of graduated values, then multiplying the Net value by the appropriate commission percentages. Commission rates used in this example are: 10 percent on the first $100, 12 percent on the next $200, and 15 percent on amounts over $300. The commission amount will be displayed on the Commission line in dollars and cents format.

To enter formula nine,

Place your cursor on B31 and type:

+B8	enters the value in B8 in B31
RETURN	enters the formula

To enter formula ten,

Place your cursor on B32 and type:

+B1	enters the value in B1 in B32
RETURN	enters the formula

To enter formula eleven,

Place your cursor on B33 and type:

(@MIN(E24,100)	selects the minimum value, the value in E24 or 100
*	multiplies
.10)	sales commission percentage
+	adds
(@MAX(0,@MIN(E24—100,200))	selects the maximum value from the comparison of 0 and the minimum value derived by comparing the value in E24 minus 100, and 200
*	multiplies
.12)	sales commission percentage
+	adds

(@MAX(0,E24—300)	seelects the maximum value, 0 or the value in E24 minus 300
*	multiplies
.15)	sales commission percentage
RETURN	enters the formula

To format to display in currency,

Leave your cursor on B33 and type:

/R	starts RANGE command
F	selects Format option
C	selects Currency option and displays number of decimal places: 2
RETURN	displays Range to format B33..B33
RETURN	executes the command

Your Customer Invoice and Sales Commission Report format is now complete and ready for you to type in invoicing information and sales entries.

To observe the automatic functions of your invoice sheet, type entries into the Quantity and Item No. columns. Some sample entries are contained in Figure 3.

SAVING

You may wish to save your entire worksheet. To do this leave your cursor on any location and type:

| /F | starts FILE command |
| S | selects SAVE option |

Type in name of file. Do not leave spaces between words.

| RETURN | executes the command |

PRINTING

To print out all or a portion of your worksheet, following the following directions, which are given for the Epson printer (compressed font).

Place your cursor on A1 and type:

| /P | starts PRINT command |

```
          A          B          C          D          E          F          G          H

 1 Invoice Number    12798
 2
 3 Customer Name Beaumont Co
 4      Address: SE Rollings St
 5         City: Portland
 6        State: Oregon      Zip Code:        97589
 7
 8 Salesperson No       22        Date: Jan 7, 83
 9
10    Quantity   Item No.  Description  Unit Cost   Total Cost
11 -----------------------------------------------------------------
12         12        225                   0.59        7.08
13        125        132                   2.36      295.00
14         25        255                   3.25       81.25
15         36        125                   0.25        9.00
16         48        129                   0.63       30.24
17                                         0.00        0.00
18                                         0.00        0.00
19                                         0.00        0.00
20 =================================================================
21                                  Freight:
22                                Sub Total:      422.57
23                         15     Discount:       -63.39
24                                      Net:      359.18
25                        5.4    Sales Tax:        19.40
26                                                ==============
27                              Grand Total:      378.58
28
29 Salesperson Commission Rpt.
30 ---------------------------
31 Salesperson No       22
32 Invoice Number    12798
33    Commission     42.88
34
35 --------------------------     ------------------------      ---------------------------
36 Pricing Table                  Pricing Table                 Discount Table
37 For Paper Prod      Price      For Glassware      Price       Amount       Percent
38 --------------------------     ------------------------      ---------------------------
39          0          0                 0           0                0            0
40        100       0.55               200        0.36              100           10
41        125       0.25               225        0.59              200           12
42        128       1.33               226        1.23              300           15
43        129       0.63               230        0.89              500           18
44        130       0.75               255        3.25
45        131       1.58               275        1.45
46        132       2.36               276        0.65
47        133          0               280           0
```

Figure 3

P	displays options
O	selects Options option
S	selects Setup option and displays Enter Setup String
\015	sets an Epson printer to compressed font
RETURN	accepts setup and displays options
M	selects Margin option
R	selects Right option
230	characters per line
RETURN	displays options
Q	selects Quit option and returns to main print menu
R	displays Range to print from
.	ellipsis—indicates from-to

Move cursor, with arrow keys, to last coordinate in area you wish to print. The screen will reverse to indicate the area being printed.

RETURN	executes the command
G	selects Go option and prints

To exit out of PRINT command, type:

Q	selects Quit option and exits out of PRINT command

EXERCISE SEVEN

COST RECOVERY

DESCRIPTION

In this exercise, you will use the 1-2-3 ability to select the minimum or maximum of values when compared to a fixed value. The exercise is designed to record a declining balance as entries accumulate against the fixed value. An increasing positive balance is recorded when the fixed value is surpassed.

To demonstrate 1-2-3's abilities, a Cost Recovery worksheet has been set up listing the equipment stocked by an equipment rental company. Each piece of equipment offered for rent has been listed, and the purchase price entered in the ledger. As the company receives rental income from the equipment, the cumulative amount is entered on the ledger sheet once a month. Your ledger format deducts the rental income from the purchase price of the item rented and displays the declining balance until the full cost is recovered. It then enters the above-cost profits as they accumulate. Once a month, an operation is performed to update the worksheet. This is done quickly and easily with the Keyboard Macros.

OPERATIONS PERFORMED

Setting Up The Worksheet Format

Naming Columns

Entering Mathematical Formulas

Making Worksheet Entries

Worksheet Updating

Updating Using Keyboard Macros

Saving

Printing

FUNCTIONS USED

ABS
MAX
MIN
SUM

COMMANDS USED

COPY	copies formulas
FILE	saves values
FILE	combines files
FILE	saves worksheet
PRINT	prints worksheet
RANGE	erases
RANGE	formats in integer
RANGE	centers labels
RANGE	names coordinates
REPEAT	repeats dashed lines
WORKSHEET	adjusts column width
WORKSHEET	formats in currency (global)

SETTING UP THE FORMAT

To set up your ledger sheet, use the following directions, copying Figure 1 exactly as it is illustrated, retaining exact row and column locations of all information.

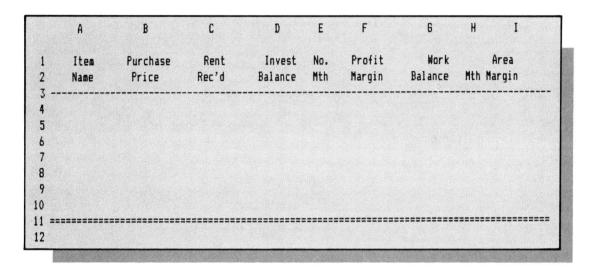

Figure 1

Enter your column headings.

After entering your column headings, you will center them in the columns by using the Center option.

Place your cursor on A1 and type:

/R	starts RANGE command
L	selects Label-Prefix option
C	selects Center option and displays Range of labels A1..A1

Move your cursor to I2. Notice the screen is reversing to show you which coordinates are to be centered.

RETURN	executes the command

To enter dashed lines on your worksheet, place your cursor on the left-most column of the row where you want the line to begin (A3 in this example.)

Type:

\	starts REPEAT command
—	label to be repeated
RETURN	executes the command

The column your cursor is on will now have a line of dashes across its width. To extend the dashed line in the same row across the remaining columns, leave your cursor where it is and type:

/C	starts COPY command and displays Range to copy from
RETURN	displays Range to copy to
B3	first coordinate to copy to
•	ellipsis—indicates from-to
I3	last coordinate to copy to
RETURN	executes the command

The dashed line will now appear extended across the columns you have indicated by your coordinates. To enter a double-dashed line on the worksheet, repeat the operations above, using the symbol = as your label to be repeated.

The 1-2-3 worksheet format contains columns nine spaces wide when it is first entered into the computer. Column width may be expanded using the following commands. In this exercise, all the columns will need to be 12 spaces wide, except for columns E and H.

First widen all your columns. Type:

/W	starts WORKSHEET command
G	selects Global option
C	selects Column-Width option

12	number of spaces in column
RETURN	executes the command

To reduce the width of column E,

Place your cursor on E1 and type:

/W	starts WORKSHEET command
C	selects Column-Width option
S	selects Set option and displays column width
4	number of spaces in column
RETURN	executes the command

To reduce the width of column H,

Place your cursor on H1 and type:

/W	starts WORKSHEET command
C	selects Column-Width option
S	selects Set option and displays column width
4	number of spaces in column
RETURN	executes the command

To format all locations to display value entries in dollars and cents, type:

/W	starts WORKSHEET command
G	selects Global option
F	selects Format option
C	selects Currency option and displays number of decimal places: 2
RETURN	executes the command

NAMING COLUMNS

Before entering mathematical formulas, you will want to name some of the column so they will be easily used in the updating process.

First name the Invest Balance, No. Mth (number of months in service) and Profit Margins columns: BALANCE. The second column to be named will be the Rent Rec'd column. The third columns to be named will be the Work Area Columns.

The first set of columns to be named are the Invest Balance, No. Mth and Profit Margins columns.

Place your cursor on D4 and type:

/R	starts RANGE command
N	selects Name option
C	selects Create option
BALANCE	name
RETURN	displays Range D4..D4

Move your cursor to F10 with the arrow keys. The screen will reverse to show the coordinates being named.

RETURN	executes the command

The second column to be named is the Rent Rec'd column.

Place your cursor on C4 and type:

/R	starts RANGE command
N	selects Name option
C	selects Create option
RENT	name
RETURN	displays Range C4..C4

Move your cursor to C10 with the arrow keys. The screen will reverse to show the coordinates being named.

RETURN	executes the command

The third set of columns to be named will be the Work Area columns.

Place your cursor on G4 and type:

/R	starts RANGE command
N	selects Name option
C	selects Create option

WORK	name
RETURN	displays Range G4..G4

Move your cursor to I10 with the arrow keys. The screen will reverse to show the coordinates being named.

| RETURN | executes the command |

ENTERING MATHEMATICAL FORMULAS

You will now begin entering mathematical formulas that will establish the relationships between column and row positions. The formulas and their locations are illustrated in Figure 2.

	A	B	C	D	E	F	G	H	I
1	Item	Purchase	Rent	Invest	No.	Profit	Work		Area
2	Name	Price	Rec'd	Balance	Mth	Margin	Balance	Mth	Margin
3	---
4		@MAX(0,G4-C4)		$0.00	1	$0.00	$0.00		
5		1+H4		$0.00	1	$0.00	$0.00		
6		@ABS(@MIN(0,G4-C4))+I4		$0.00	1	$0.00	$0.00		
7		+B4		$0.00	1	$0.00	$0.00		
8				$0.00	1	$0.00	$0.00		
9				$0.00	1	$0.00	$0.00		
10				$0.00	1	$0.00	$0.00		
11	===
12	@SUM(B3.B11)	$0.00	$0.00	$0.00		$0.00			

Figure 2

Formula one provides a means for the Invest Balance column to display the unrecovered purchase cost of each item listed. When the full purchase cost of each piece of equipment is recovered, the Invest Balance column will display 0.00 opposite that item.

Place your cursor on D4 and type:

@MAX(0,G4-C4)	selects the maximum value, 0, or the result of Work Area balance minus Rent Rec'd
RETURN	enters the formula

Formula two advances the number in the No. Mths column by one each time the updating operating is performed.

Place your cursor on E4 and type:

1+H4	adds 1 to the Work Area Month
RETURN	enters the formula

To format column E to display values in integers, type:

/R	starts RANGE command
F	selects Format option
G	selects General option
RETURN	executes the command

Formula three displays accumulated gross profits in the Profit Margin column when purchase cost of the listed item has been recovered.

Place your cursor on F4 and type:

@ABS	reads the answer to the following calculation as an absolute function
(@MIN(0,G4-C4))	selects the minimum value, 0, or the result of Work Area balance minus Rent Rec'd
+I4	adds Work Area Margin to the value selected by the MIN formula
RETURN	enters the formula

Formula four displays the original purchase price in a Work Area Balance column.

Place your cursor on G4 and type:

+B4	enters the Purchase Price
RETURN	enters the formula

Your next operation is to copy the formulas just entered at the top of each column into each row in the respective columns.

Place your cursor on D4 and type:

/C	starts COPY command and displays Range to copy from
D4	first coordinate to copy from
.	ellipsis—indicates from-to
G4	last coordinate to copy from
RETURN	displays Range to copy to
D5	first coordinate to copy to
.	ellipsis—indicates from-to
D10	last coordinate to copy to
RETURN	executes the command

Formula five displays the sum of the entries in each column. It is necessary to enter a formula at the bottom that will add the values.

Place your cursor on B12 and type:

@SUM(	adds values in the list
B3	first coordinate of column to add
.	ellipsis—indicates from-to
B11)	last coordinate of column to add
RETURN	enters the formula

Your next operation is to copy the formula just entered at the bottom of each column you wish to add.

Leave your cursor on B12 and type:

/C	starts COPY command and displays range to copy from
RETURN	displays Range to copy to
C12	first coordinate to copy to
.	ellipsis—indicates from-to

F12   last coordinate to copy to

RETURN   executes the command

You won't need the SUM formula at the bottom of the No. Mths column, so place your cursor on E12 and type:

/R   starts RANGE command

E   selects Erase option

RETURN   executes the command

MAKING WORKSHEET ENTRIES

Your Cost Recovery Ledger is now set up so once a month all you have to do is perform the update process, described in the next section, and make current billing entries. To get your ledger operational, type in the entries in the Item Name, Purchase Price and Rent Rec'd columns in Figure 3 exactly as they are shown.

	A	B	C	D	E	F	G	H	I
1	Item	Purchase	Rent	Invest	No.	Profit	Work		Area
2	Name	Price	Rec'd	Balance	Mth	Margin	Balance	Mth	Margin
3	--
4	Hammer	$25.00	$5.00	$20.00	1	$0.00	$25.00		
5	Trailer	$675.00	$155.00	$520.00	1	$0.00	$675.00		
6	Shovel	$55.00	$89.00	$0.00	1	$34.00	$55.00		
7	Bike	$255.00	$15.00	$240.00	1	$0.00	$255.00		
8	Truck	$6,500.00	$250.00	$6,250.00	1	$0.00	$6,500.00		
9	Motor	$152.00	$225.00	$0.00	1	$73.00	$152.00		
10	Ax	$89.00	$18.00	$71.00	1	$0.00	$89.00		
11	==
12		$7,751.00	$757.00	$7,101.00		$107.00			

Figure 3

LEDGER UPDATING

The first operation in the updating process is to save the values in the Invest Balance, No. Mths and Profit Margin columns under the name BALANCE into a storage file on a disk. Before loading the file back onto the area you will need to erase the Work Area columns because 1-2-3 does not copy blanks. Then the BALANCE file will be loaded onto the worksheet in the Work Area columns. The last operation will be to erase the Rent Rec'd column from your worksheet to get ready for the next month's entries.

First you will save the columns named BALANCE (Invest Balance, No. Mth and Profit Margin columns) into a filename called BALANCE. To do this, type:

/F	starts FILE command
X	selects Xtract option
V	selects Value option which saves only the values
BALANCE	filename
RETURN	displays Range
BALANCE	name of columns
RETURN	executes the command

Second operation is to erase the Work Area columns. To do this type:

/R	starts RANGE command
E	selects Erase option
WORK	name of Range to erase
RETURN	executes the command

Your third operation will be to combine the file named BALANCE onto the worksheet into the Work Area columns.

Place your cursor on G4 and type:

/F	starts FILE command
C	selects Combine option
C	selects Copy option
E	selects Entire File option

BALANCE	filename
RETURN	executes the command

The last operation in the updating procedure will be to erase the Rent Rec'd column. Type:

/R	starts RANGE command
E	selects Erase option
RENT	name of coordinates
RETURN	executes the command

Your ledger sheet should now look exactly like Figure 4 and ready for next month's entries.

	A	B	C	D	E	F	G	H	I
1	Item	Purchase	Rent	Invest	No.	Profit	Work		Area
2	Name	Price	Rec'd	Balance	Mth	Margin	Balance	Mth	Margin
3	--
4	Hammer	$25.00		$20.00	2	$0.00	$20.00	1	$0.00
5	Trailer	$675.00		$520.00	2	$0.00	$520.00	1	$0.00
6	Shovel	$55.00		$0.00	2	$34.00	$0.00	1	$34.00
7	Bike	$255.00		$240.00	2	$0.00	$240.00	1	$0.00
8	Truck	$6,500.00		$6,250.00	2	$0.00	$6,250.00	1	$0.00
9	Motor	$152.00		$0.00	2	$73.00	$0.00	1	$73.00
10	Ax	$89.00		$71.00	2	$0.00	$71.00	1	$0.00
11	==
12		$7,751.00	$0.00	$7,101.00		$107.00			

Figure 4

UPDATING WITH KEYBOARD MACROS

1-2-3 has an extremely powerful feature which is called Keyboard Macros, which allows you to set up a string of keystroke information in a small file, enabling you to perform an operation, such as the worksheet updating we just did, with a single keystroke.

To set up the Keyboard Macros, you will first need to enter the keystroke information into a coordinate or a group of adjacent coordinates in a column.

Next you will need to name the coordinate or group of coordinates which contain the keystroke information, using a backslash followed by any single character from A to Z. Example: \A

First we will enter the Keyboard Macros file.

_____ NOTE _____

An apostrophe (') is entered at the beginning of each line to prepare coordinates for label information.

The ˜ represents a RETURN.

We have put an r after the filename RETURN because the computer asks if you want to Replace or Cancel a file which already exists on the disk. The R represents the Replace.

{goto} moves cursor to the coordinate following it.

_____

To enter the Keyboard Macros file,

Place your cursor on A17 and type:

, /fxvBALANCE˜BALANCE˜r
, /reWORK˜
, {goto}G4˜
, /fcceBALANCE˜
, /reRENT˜

Second operation will be to name the coordinates containing the Keyboard Macros.

Place your cursor on A17 and type:

/R	starts RANGE command
N	selects Name option
C	selects Create option

| \A | name of coordinate |
| RETURN | displays Range: A17..A17 |

Move your cursor to A21 with the arrow keys. The screen will reverse to show coordinates being named.

| RETURN | executes the command |

Now that the keyboard macros file is named, to demonstrate its use, first enter new Rent Rec'd information as illustrated in Figure 5.

	A	B	C	D	E	F	G	H	I
1	Item	Purchase	Rent	Invest	No.	Profit	Work		Area
2	Name	Price	Rec'd	Balance	Mth	Margin	Balance	Mth	Margin
3	--
4	Hammer	$25.00	$35.00	$0.00	2	$15.00	$20.00	1	$0.00
5	Trailer	$675.00	$200.00	$320.00	2	$0.00	$520.00	1	$0.00
6	Shovel	$55.00	$20.00	$0.00	2	$54.00	$0.00	1	$34.00
7	Bike	$255.00		$240.00	2	$0.00	$240.00	1	$0.00
8	Truck	$6,500.00	$2,500.00	$3,750.00	2	$0.00	$6,250.00	1	$0.00
9	Motor	$152.00	$25.00	$0.00	2	$98.00	$0.00	1	$73.00
10	Ax	$89.00	$45.00	$26.00	2	$0.00	$71.00	1	$0.00
11	==
12		$7,751.00	$2,825.00	$4,336.00		$167.00			
13									
14									
15									
16									
17	/fxvBALANCE~BALANCE~r								
18	/reWORK~								
19	{goto}G4~								
20	/fcceBALANCE~								
21	/reRENT~								

Figure 5

To execute the macros:

Hold the Alt key down and press A.

Sit back and watch what happens. Your worksheet should look like Figure 6.

	A	B	C	D	E	F	G	H	I
1	Item	Purchase	Rent	Invest	No.	Profit	Work		Area
2	Name	Price	Rec'd	Balance	Mth	Margin	Balance	Mth	Margin
3	--								
4	Hammer	$25.00		$0.00	3	$15.00	$0.00	2	$15.00
5	Trailer	$675.00		$320.00	3	$0.00	$320.00	2	$0.00
6	Shovel	$55.00		$0.00	3	$54.00	$0.00	2	$54.00
7	Bike	$255.00		$240.00	3	$0.00	$240.00	2	$0.00
8	Truck	$6,500.00		$3,750.00	3	$0.00	$3,750.00	2	$0.00
9	Motor	$152.00		$0.00	3	$98.00	$0.00	2	$98.00
10	Ax	$89.00		$26.00	3	$0.00	$26.00	2	$0.00
11	==								
12		$7,751.00	$0.00	$4,336.00		$167.00			
13									
14									
15									
16									
17	/fxvBALANCE~BALANCE~r								
18	/reWORK~								
19	{goto}G4~								
20	/fcceBALANCE~								
21	/reRENT~								

Figure 6

SAVING

You may wish to save your entire worksheet. To do this leave your cursor on any location and type:

/F	starts FILE command
S	selects SAVE option

Type in name of file. Do not leave spaces between words.

RETURN	executes the command

PRINTING

To print out all or a portion of your worksheet, use the following directions, which are given for the Epson printer (compressed font).

Place your cursor on A1 and type:

/P	starts PRINT command
P	displays options
O	selects Options option
S	selects Setup option and displays Enter Setup String
\ 015	sets an Epson printer to compressed font
RETURN	accepts setup and displays options
M	selects Margin option
R	selects Right option
230	characters per line
RETURN	displays options
Q	selects Quit option and returns to main print menu
R	displays Range to print from
.	ellipsis—indicates from-to

Move cursor, with arrow keys, to last coordinate in area you wish to print. The screen will reverse to indicate the area being printed.

RETURN   executes the command

G   selects Go option and prints

To exit out of PRINT command, type:

Q   selects Quit option and exits
                                    out of PRINT command

EXERCISE EIGHT

PRODUCTION SCHEDULING

DESCRIPTION

The Lotus 1-2-3 program abilities to determine a date, move information from one area of a worksheet to another for recalculation, and view two areas of a worksheet at the same time by using a split-screen, are employed in this exercise.

To demonstrate these abilities, a production schedule worksheet for a stained glass lamp manufacturer has been set up. The schedule contains three weeks of plant production and a summary of those weeks. Monday's date for each week is determined and displayed by the Date function. As you enter information into your weekly schedule, you will also be able to view your summary totals by using the split-screen capability. Then you will be able to move information from one week to another, and recalculate the weekly totals.

OPERATIONS PERFORMED

Setting Up The Worksheet Format

Entering Mathematical Formulas

Making Scheduling Sheet Entries

Rescheduling Entries

Saving

Printing

FUNCTIONS

AVERAGE
DATE
SUM

COMMANDS USED

COPY	copies formulas
FILE	saves worksheet
MOVE	repositions item on worksheet
PRINT	prints worksheet
RANGE	formats in Date format
RANGE	centers labels
RANGE	formats in integer
REPEAT	repeats dashed lines
WORKSHEET	splits screen
WORKSHEET	deletes row
WORKSHEET	inserts row
WORKSHEET	adjusts column width (global)
WORKSHEET	adjusts column width (column)

SETTING UP THE WORKSHEET FORMAT

To set up your production scheduling sheet, use the following directions, copying Figure 1 exactly as it is illustrated, retaining exact row and column locations of all information.

Enter your column headings.

After entering your column headings, you will center them in the columns by using the Center option.

Place your cursor on A5 and type:

/R	starts RANGE command
L	selects Label—Prefix option
C	selects Center option and displays Range of labels A5..A5

Move your cursor to I6. Notice the screen is reversing to show you which coordinates are to be centered.

RETURN	executes the command

To enter dashed lines on your worksheet, place your cursor on the left-most column of the row where you want the line to begin (A2 in this example.)

Type:

\	starts REPEAT command
—	label to be repeated
RETURN	executes the command

The column your cursor is on will now have a line of dashes across its width. To extend the dashed line in the same row across the remaining columns, leave your cursor where it is and type:

/C	starts COPY command and displays Range to copy from
RETURN	displays Range to copy to
B2	first coordinate to copy to
•	ellipsis—indicates from-to
I2	last coordinate to copy to
RETURN	executes the command

```
          A        B        C        D        E        F        G        H        I

 1 Max Number of Shop Hours in a Week=    200
 2 -----------------------------------------------------------------------------
 3 Year            83   Month          Mon.Date
 4 -----------------------------------------------------------------------------
 5   Job    Customer  Pattern   Cut    Assem-    Ship    Est.    PCT of  Hrs vs
 6 Number     Name    Making   Glass    ble              Hours   Max Hrs Max Hrs
 7 -----------------------------------------------------------------------------
 8
 9
10
11 ============================================================================
12 Totals
13 -----------------------------------------------------------------------------
14
15 -----------------------------------------------------------------------------
16   Job    Customer  Pattern   Cut    Assem-    Ship    Est.    PCT of  Hrs vs
17 Number     Name    Making   Glass    ble              Hours   Max Hrs
18 -----------------------------------------------------------------------------
19
20
21
22 ============================================================================
23 Totals
24 -----------------------------------------------------------------------------
25
26 -----------------------------------------------------------------------------
27   Job    Customer  Pattern   Cut    Assem-    Ship    Est.    PCT of  Hrs vs
28 Number     Name    Making   Glass    ble              Hours   Max Hrs Max Hrs
29 -----------------------------------------------------------------------------
30
31
32
33 ============================================================================
34 Totals
35 -----------------------------------------------------------------------------
36 Plant Production Summary
37 -----------------------------------------------------------------------------
38 Monday's          Pattern   Cut    Assem-    Ship    Est.    PCT of  Hrs vs
39 Date              Making   Glass    ble              Hours   Max Hrs Max Hrs
40 -----------------------------------------------------------------------------
41
42
43
44 ============================================================================
45 Totals
46
```

Figure 1

The dashed line will now appear extended across the columns you have indicated by your coordinates. To enter a double-dashed line on the worksheet, repeat the operations above, using the symbol = as your label to be repeated.

The 1-2-3 worksheet format contains columns nine spaces wide when it is first entered into the computer. The columns widths in this exercise needed to be changed.

First reduce all your columns. Type:

/W	starts WORKSHEET command
G	selects Global option
C	selects Column-Width option
8	number of spaces in column
RETURN	executes the command

Next reduce column A to 7 spaces.

Place your cursor on A1 and type:

/W	starts WORKSHEET command
C	selects Column-Width option
S	selects Set option and displays column width
7	number of spaces in column
RETURN	executes the command

Next expand column B to 12 spaces. Type:

/W	starts WORKSHEET command
C	selects Column-Width option
S	selects Set option and displays column width
12	number of spaces in column
RETURN	executes the command

ENTERING MATHEMATICAL FORMULAS

You will now begin entering mathematical formulas which will establish the relationships between column and row positions. The formulas and their positions are illustrated in Figure 2.

Your first formula will total the estimated hours from the Pattern Making, Cut Glass, Assemble and Ship columns in the Est. Hours column.

Place your cursor on G8 and type:

@SUM(	adds values in the list
C8	first coordinate of column to add
.	ellipsis—indicates from-to
F8)	last coordinate of column to add
RETURN	enters the formula

Formula two calculates the percent each work order represents of the maximum hours available in the week by dividing the Est. Hours column total for individual work orders by the maximum hours available. The result is multiplied by 100 to display the percentage value as a whole number.

NOTE

1-2-3 is designed to do one of two things with coordinates when they are copied. The coordinates are either relative to their new location or they remain absolute, which means they remain the same.

A coordinate address is relative unless it is converted to an absolute by having a dollar sign ($) preceding the column designation and/or row designation, i.e., ($G$8).

A quick way to make a coordinate absolute is by putting the cursor on that coordinate and pressing the F4 key, which will place the dollar as shown automatically.

To enter formula two,

Place your cursor on H8 and type:

+	prepares coordinate to accept a numeric expression
G8	coordinate containing estimated hours

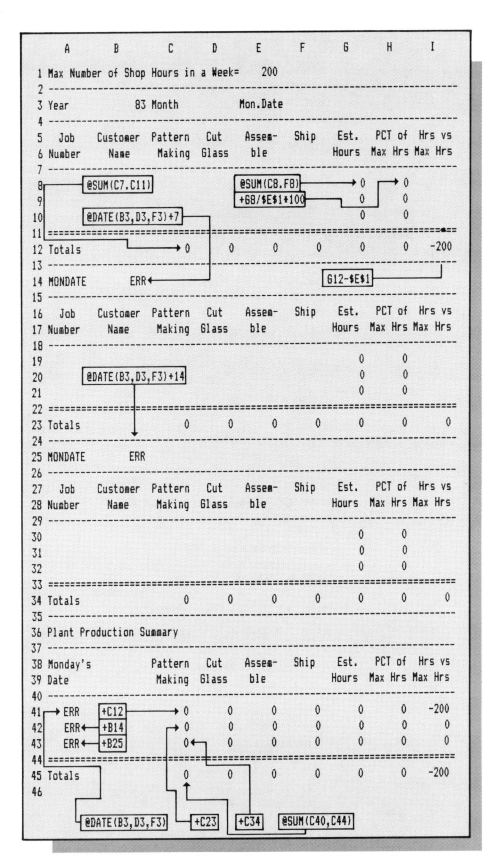

Figure 2

/	divides
$E$1	coordinate containing maximum number of shop hours in a week Note: $ converts coordinate to absolute address
*	multiplies
100	value
RETURN	enters the formula

A division by zero displays ERR until a value is entered into E1.
To format to display as an integer, leave your cursor on H8 and type:

/R	starts RANGE command
F	selects Format option
G	selects General option
RETURN	displays Range to format H8..H8
RETURN	executes the command

Your next operation is to copy the formulas just entered into the remaining rows in their respective columns down to the dashed line.

Leave your cursor on H8 and type:

/C	starts COPY command and displays Range to copy from
G8	first coordinate to copy from
•	ellipsis—indicates from-to
H8	last coordinate to copy from
RETURN	displays Range to copy to
G9	first coordinate to copy to
•	ellipsis—indicates from-to
G10	last coordinate to copy to
RETURN	executes the command

Formula three will add the total of values in the PATTERN MAKING column.

Place your cursor on C12 and type:

@SUM(	adds values in the list
C7	first coordinate of column to add
•	ellipsis—indicates from-to
C11)	last coordinate of column to add
RETURN	enters the formula

Your next operation is to copy the formula just entered at the bottom of each column you wish to add.

Leave your cursor on C12 and type:

/C	starts COPY command and displays Range to copy from
RETURN	displays Range to copy to
D12	first coordinate to copy to
•	ellipsis—indicates from-to
H12	last coordinate to copy to
RETURN	executes the command

Formula four will compare the total estimated hours against the maximum shop hours available and display the difference at the bottom of the Hrs vs Max Hrs column. A negative value indicates hours remaining; a positive value, hours exceeded.

NOTE

1-2-3 is designed to do one of two things with coordinates when they are copied. The coordinates are either relative to their new location or they remain absolute, which means they remain the same.

A coordinate address is relative unless it is converted to an absolute by having a dollar sign ($) preceding the column designation and/or row designation, i.e. ($G$8).

A quick way to make a coordinate absolute is by placing your cursor on that coordinate and pressing the F4 key, which will place the dollar as shown automatically.

Place your cursor on I12 and type:

+	prepares coordinate to accept a numeric expression
G12	coordinate containing estimated hours
—	subtracts
$E$1	coordinate containing maximum number of shop hours in a week Note: $ converts coordinate to an absolute address
RETURN	enters the formula

The next operation is to copy the formulas just entered into the first week into week two. To do this,

Leave your cursor on any location and type:

/C	starts COPY command and displays Range to copy from
A4	first coordinate to copy from
.	ellipsis—indicates from-to
I12	last coordinate to copy from
RETURN	displays Range to copy to
A15	first coordinate to copy to
RETURN	executes the command

The next operation is to copy the formulas into the third week. To do this, leave your cursor on any location and type:

/C	starts COPY command and displays Range to copy from
A4	first coordinate to copy from
.	ellipsis—indicates from-to
I12	last coordinate to copy from
RETURN	displays Range to copy to
A26	first coordinate to copy to
RETURN	executes the command

In Formula five, in Row 14, you will first enter the label, MONDATE, in A14; and the formula to calculate second week's Monday's date, in B14.

To enter the label place your cursor on A14 and type:

MONDATE	label
RETURN	enters the label

To enter formula five, place your cursor on B14 and type:

@DATE(	starts DATE function
B3,	coordinate containing year
D3,	coordinate containing month
F3)	coordinate containing Mon.Date
+	adds
7	number of days in week
RETURN	enters the formula

Next operation is to format the formula just entered to convert the absolute number generated by the formula to read in day and month.

Leave your cursor on B14 and type:

/R	starts RANGE command
F	selects Format option
D	selects Date format
2	selects (DD-MMM) and displays Range to format: B14..B14
RETURN	executes the command

In Formula six, in Row 25, you will first enter the label, MONDATE, in A25, and the formula to calculate second week's Monday's date, in B25.

To enter the label place your cursor on A25 and type:

MONDATE	label
RETURN	enters the label

To enter formula six, place your cursor on B25 and type:

@DATE(	starts DATE function
B3,	coordinate containing year
D3,	coordinate containing month
F3)	coordinate containing Mon.Date
+	adds
14	number of days in two weeks
RETURN	enters the formula

Next operation is to format the formula just entered to convert the absolute number generated by the formula to read in day and month.

Leave your cursor on B25 and type:

/R	starts RANGE command
F	selects Format option
D	selects Date format
2	selects (DD-MMM) and displays Range to format: B25..B25
RETURN	executes the command

Formulas seven, eight and nine display Monday's Date in the appropriate columns in the Plant Production Summary.

To enter formula seven, place your cursor on A41 and type:

@DATE(	starts DATE function
B3,	coordinate containing year
D3,	coordinate containing month
F3)	coordinate containing Mon.Date
RETURN	enters the formula

To enter formula eight, place your cursor on A42 and type:

+	prepares coordinate to accept a numeric expression

B14	coordinate containing second week's MON DATE
RETURN	enters the formula

To enter formula nine, place your cursor on A43 and type:

+	prepares coordinate to accept a numeric expression
B25	coordinate containing third week's MON DATE
RETURN	enters the formula

To convert the three previous formulas to read the absolute value out in Day and Month format, leave your cursor on A43 and type:

/R	starts RANGE command
F	selects Format option
D	selects Date format
2	selects (DD-MMM) format and displays Range to format: A43..A43

Move your cursor to A41 with the arrow keys. Screen will reverse to indicate which coordinates are being formatted.

RETURN	executes the command

Formulas ten, eleven and twelve, in the Plant Production Summary, transfers Pattern Making Totals from the weekly production schedule totals.

To enter formula ten, place your cursor on C41 and type:

+	prepares coordinate to accept a numeric expression
C12	coordinate containing Pattern Making Total
RETURN	enters the formula

To enter formula eleven, place your cursor on C42 and type:

+	prepares the coordinate to accept a numeric expression

C23	coordinate containing Pattern Making Total
RETURN	enters the formula

To enter formula twelve, place your cursor on C43 and type:

+	prepares coordinate to accept a numeric expression
C34	coordinate containing Pattern Making Total
RETURN	enters the formula

Formula thirteen, adds the Pattern Making Totals.

To enter formula thirteen, place your cursor on C45 and type:

@SUM(	adds values in the following list
C40	first coordinate of row to add
•	ellipsis—indicates from-to
C44)	last coordinate of row to add
RETURN	enters the formula

Now copy the prior four formulas entered, formulas ten through thirteen, into appropriate positions in columns to the right.

Leave your cursor on any location and type:

/C	selects COPY command and displays Range to copy from
C41	first coordinate to copy from
•	ellipsis—indicates from-to
C45	last coordinate to copy from
RETURN	displays Range to copy to
D41	first coordinate to copy to
•	ellipsis—indicates from-to
I41	last coordinate to copy to
RETURN	executes the command

Formula fourteen replaces the SUM formula in coordinate H45 with the AVERAGE function to obtain the correct percentage rate of maximum hours used.

Place your cursor on H45 and type:

@AVG(	averages values in the following list
H41	first coordinate in the list
.	ellipsis—indicates from-to
H43)	last coordinate in the list
RETURN	enters the formula

MAKING SCHEDULING SHEET ENTRIES

Your production scheduling sheet is now ready for use. To perform the following operations, type in the entries in Figure 3 exactly as they are shown.

RESCHEDULING ENTRIES

Your entire production scheduling sheet cannot be viewed on your computer screen because it is too long. To allow you to view the Plant Production Summary as you move work orders from one week to another for rescheduling, you will now utilize the WINDOW option to split the screen horizontally in two. The Plant Production Summary will be displayed in the lower window, and will remain stationary. The upper window will be used to scan the entire production scheduling sheet, selecting portions where changes will be made. The split window format is illustrated in Figures 4-A and 4-B.

Position line 46 as the last line displayed on your screen. This will position your Plant Production Summary in the lower half of your screen.

Place your cursor on A35 and type:

/W	starts WORKSHEET command
W	selects Window option
H	selects Horizontal option

———————————— **NOTE** ————————————

Your cursor will be located in the upper window. You may move it from one window to the other by depressing the F6 key.

```
        A         B        C        D         E        F        G        H         I

 1 Max Number of Shop Hours in a Week=    200
 2 ----------------------------------------------------------------------------
 3 Year             83   Month       7 Mon.Date     5
 4 ----------------------------------------------------------------------------
 5   Job    Customer  Pattern   Cut    Assem-    Ship    Est.   PCT of  Hrs vs
 6 Number     Name    Making   Glass    ble            Hours   Max Hrs Max Hrs
 7 ----------------------------------------------------------------------------
 8   1258 Williams       12      23       12       2      49    24.5
 9    598 Tiffany        56      30        6       1      93    46.5
10   4578 Tyler          45      18       12     1.5    76.5   38.25
11 ============================================================================
12 Totals               113      71       30     4.5   218.5  109.25    18.5
13 ----------------------------------------------------------------------------
14 MON.DAT     12-Jul
15 ----------------------------------------------------------------------------
16   Job    Customer  Pattern   Cut    Assem-    Ship    Est.   PCT of  Hrs vs
17 Number     Name    Making   Glass    ble            Hours   Max Hrs Max Hrs
18 ----------------------------------------------------------------------------
19    223 Sitton         15      31       14       1      61    30.5
20    369 Phillips       12      32       24       1      69    34.5
21    897 Gold           53      10       13     1.5    77.5   38.75
22 ============================================================================
23 Totals                80      73       51     3.5   207.5  103.75     7.5
24 ----------------------------------------------------------------------------
25 MON.DAT     19-Jul
26 ----------------------------------------------------------------------------
27   Job    Customer  Pattern   Cut    Assem-    Ship    Est.   PCT of  Hrs vs
28 Number     Name    Making   Glass    ble            Hours   Max Hrs Max Hrs
29 ----------------------------------------------------------------------------
30    988 Mackey         12      16       10       1      39    19.5
31    334 Raleigh        13      14        5     0.5    32.5   16.25
32    721 Pedrone        13      19       12       2      46      23
33 ============================================================================
34 Totals                38      49       27     3.5   117.5   58.75   -82.5
35 ----------------------------------------------------------------------------
36 Plant Production Summary
37 ----------------------------------------------------------------------------
38 Monday's            Pattern   Cut    Assem-    Ship    Est.   PCT of  Hrs vs
39 Date                Making   Glass    ble            Hours   Max Hrs Max Hrs
40 ----------------------------------------------------------------------------
41 05-Jul               113      71       30     4.5   218.5  109.25    18.5
42 12-Jul                80      73       51     3.5   207.5  103.75     7.5
43 19-Jul                38      49       27     3.5   117.5   58.75   -82.5
44 ============================================================================
45 Totals               231     193      108    11.5   543.5 90.5833   -56.5
46
```

Figure 3

To demonstrate how the production scheduling sheet recalculates values when a work order is moved for rescheduling, move the Tiffany order from week one to week three.

Before the move, your worksheet should look like Figure 4-A.

Before starting the MOVE command, you must insert a Row.

Place your cursor on A31 and type:

/W	starts WORKSHEET command
I	selects Insert option
R	selects Row option
RETURN	executes the command

To execute the move,

Place your cursor on A9 and type:

/M	starts MOVE command and displays Range to move: A9..A9

Move your cursor to H9 with arrow. Screen will reverse to display area being moved.

RETURN	displays Range to move to
A31	Range to move to
RETURN	executes the command

Your worksheet should look like Figure 4-B.

If you wish, you may delete Row 9 which is now blank. To do this, type:

/W	starts WORKSHEET command
D	selects Delete option
R	selects Row option
RETURN	executes the command

8 EXERCISE Production Scheduling

	A	B	C	D	E	F	G	H
6	Number	Name	Making	Glass	ble		Hours	Max Hrs
7	------	--------	------	-----	----	---	------	-------
8	1258	Williams	12	23	12	2	49	24.5
9	598	Tiffany	56	30	6	1	93	46.5
10	4578	Tyler	45	18	12	1.5	76.5	38.25
11	======	========	======	=====	====	===	======	=======
12	Totals		113	71	30	4.5	218.5	109.25
13	------	--------	------	-----	----	---	------	-------

	A	B	C	D	E	F	G	H
36	-------	--------	-------	-----	------	----	-----	-------
37	Plant Production Summary							
38	-------	--------	-------	-----	------	----	-----	-------
39	Monday's		Pattern	Cut	Assem-	Ship	Est.	PCT of
40	Date		Making	Glass	ble		Hours	Max Hrs
41	-------	--------	-------	-----	------	----	-----	-------
42	07-Jul		113	71	30	4.5	218.5	109.25
43	14-Jul		80	73	51	3.5	207.5	104.25
44	21-Jul		38	49	27	3.5	117.5	58.75
45	=======	========	=======	=====	======	====	=====	=======
46	Totals		231	193	108	11.5	543.5	90.75

Before the move

Figure 4-A

	A	B	C	D	E	F	G	H
28	Number	Name	Making	Glass	ble		Hours	Max Hrs
29	------	-------	------	-----	----	---	------	-------
30	988	Mackey	12	16	10	1	39	19.5
31	598	Tiffany	56	30	6	1	93	46.5
32	334	Raleigh	13	14	5	0.5	32.5	16.25
33	721	Pedrone	13	19	12	2	46	23
34	======	=======	======	=====	====	===	======	=======
35	Totals		94	79	33	4.5	210.5	105.25

	A	B	C	D	E	F	G	H
36	-------	--------	-------	-----	------	----	-----	-------
37	Plant Production Summary							
38	-------	--------	-------	-----	------	----	-----	-------
39	Monday's		Pattern	Cut	Assem-	Ship	Est.	PCT of
40	Date		Making	Glass	ble		Hours	Max Hrs
41	-------	--------	-------	-----	------	----	-----	-------
42	07-Jul		57	41	24	3.5	125.5	62.75
43	14-Jul		80	73	51	3.5	207.5	104.25
44	21-Jul		94	79	33	4.5	210.5	105.25
45	=======	========	=======	=====	======	====	=====	=======
46	Totals		231	193	108	11.5	543.5	90.75

After the move

Figure 4-B

SAVING

You may wish to save your entire worksheet. To do this leave your cursor on any location and type:

/F	starts FILE command
S	selects SAVE option

Type in name of file. Do not leave spaces between words.

RETURN	executes the command

PRINTING

To print out all or a portion of your worksheet, use the following directions, which are given for the Epson printer (compressed font).

Place your cursor on A1 and type:

/P	starts PRINT command
P	displays options
O	selects Options option
S	selects Setup option and displays Enter Setup String
\015	sets an Epson printer to compressed font
RETURN	accepts setup and displays options
M	selects Margin option
R	selects Right option
230	characters per line
RETURN	displays options
Q	selects Quit option and returns to main print menu
R	displays Range to print from
•	ellipsis—indicates from-to

Move cursor, with arrow keys, to last coordinate in area you wish to print. The screen will reverse to indicate the area being printed.

RETURN   executes the command

G   selects Go option and prints

To exit out of PRINT command, type:

Q   selects Quit option and exits
                                out of PRINT command

EXERCISE NINE

DAILY INVENTORY

DESCRIPTION

The Lotus 1-2-3 program has the ability to sort information in ascending or descending order, and move information from one area of the worksheet to another for updating purposes.

To demonstrate this, a daily inventory report worksheet has been set up. Updating is done on a daily basis. This operation is performed with a single keystroke using the Keyboard Macros. A code is set up to determine when to reorder a particular product, and, after entering of inventory information, you will sort it by Item number, in ascending order.

OPERATIONS PERFORMED

Setting Up The Worksheet Format

Entering Mathematical Formulas

Making Worksheet Entries

Sorting Numbers in Ascending Order

Daily Updating

Clearing Worksheet Entries

Updating, Using Keyboard Macros

Saving

Printing

FUNCTIONS USED

IF
MAX
NA
SUM
TRUE

COMMANDS USED

COPY	copies formulas
DATA	sorts items
FILE	saves values
FILE	saves worksheet
FILE	combines files
PRINT	prints worksheet
RANGE	erases
RANGE	names coordinates
RANGE	formats in currency
RANGE	centers labels
REPEAT	repeats dashed lines
WORKSHEET	adjusts column width

SETTING UP THE WORKSHEET FORMAT

The worksheet that you will set up consists of the DAILY INVENTORY REPORT. To set up this worksheet, use the following instructions, copying Figure 1 exactly as it is illustrated, retaining exact row and column locations of all information.

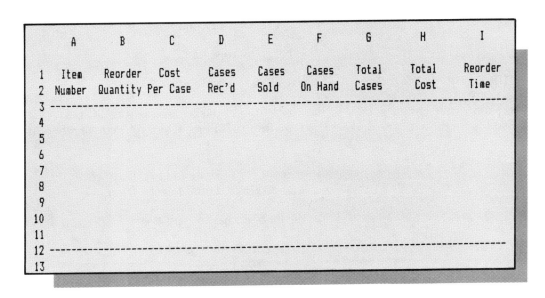

Figure 1

Enter your column headings.

After entering your column headings, you will center them in the columns by using the Center option.

Place your cursor on A1 and type:

/R	starts RANGE command
L	selects Label-Prefix option
C	selects Center option and displays Range of labels A1..A1

Move your cursor to I2. Notice the screen is reversing to show you which coordinates are to be centered.

RETURN	executes the command

To enter dashed lines on your worksheet, place your cursor on the left-most column of the row where you want the line to begin (A3 in this example.)

Type:

\	starts REPEAT command
—	label to be repeated
RETURN	executes the command

The column your cursor is on will now have line of dashes across its width. To extend the dashed line in the same row across the remaining columns, leave your cursor where it is and type:

/C	starts COPY command and displays Range to copy from
RETURN	displays Range to copy to
B3	first coordinate to copy to
.	ellipsis—indicates from-to
I3	last coordinate to copy to
RETURN	executes the command

The dashed line will now appear extended across the columns you have indicated by your coordinates. To enter a double-dashed line on the worksheet, repeat the operations above, using the symbol = as your label to be repeated.

The 1-2-3 worksheet format contains columns nine spaces wide when it is first entered into the computer. Column width may be expanded using the following commands. In this exercise, column H will have to be expanded to accommodate large numbers.

To expand column H, place your cursor on H1 and type:

/W	starts WORKSHEET command
C	selects Column-Width option
S	selects Set option and displays column width

12	number of spaces in column
RETURN	executes the command

ENTERING MATHEMATICAL FORMULAS

You will now begin entering mathematical formulas that will establish the relationship between column and row locations. The formulas and their locations are illustrated in Figure 2.

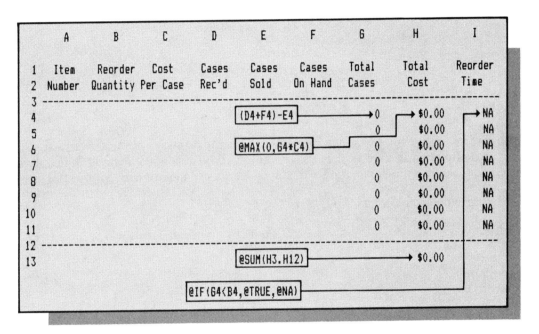

Figure 2

Formula one, adds, in the same row, the Cases Rec'd column and the Cases On Hand column and, from that total, subtracts the Cases Sold column, in the same row. The value generated is then displayed in the Total Cases column of the same row.

Place your cursor on G4 and type:

(	opens expression
D4	coordinate containing cases received
+	adds
F4	coordinate containing cases on hand
)	closes expression
—	subtracts
E4	coordinate containing cases sold
RETURN	enters the formula

Formula two, in the Total Cost column, determines the total cost of each inventory item. The MAX logic function is used so that a zero value will be displayed if the item is out of stock. Otherwise, a minus amount could be displayed, because a negative amount would be totaled.

Place your cursor on H4 and type:

@MAX	selects the maximum value of the following list
(	opens the list
0	value in the list
,	comma—separates values in the list
G4	coordinate containing total cases
*	multiplies
C4	coordinate containing cost per case
)	closes the list
RETURN	enters the formula

To format in dollars and cents, type:

/R	starts RANGE command
F	selects Format option

C	selects Currency option and displays # of decimal places: 2
RETURN	displays Range to format H4..H4
RETURN	executes the command

Formula three, in the Reorder Time column, uses IF logic function to determine if it is time to reorder an item. If it is time to reorder, it displays the word TRUE: if not, it displays NA.

_____ **NOTE** _____

IF logic function contains three expressions separated by commas. The first expression generates a true or false value as a result of a logical operation. If the value is true, the IF selects the value generated by the second expression. If the value is false, the IF selects the value generated by the third expression.

_____

Place your cursor on I4 and type:

@IF(	starts IF logic function
G4	part of the first expression, which generates the first value to be compared
<	Logical Operator, compares the first value against the second value and results in the logical value of true or false
B4	coordinate containing the second value to be compared
,	comma-separates expressions in the IF function
@TRUE	TRUE function produces a logical value TRUE, which is the second expression in the IF function and which will be selected if the first expression is true
,	comma-separates expressions in the IF function

9 EXERCISE Daily Inventory

@NA	NA function produces a logical value NA, which is the third expression of the IF function, which will be selected if the first expression is false
)	closes IF logic function
RETURN	enters the formula

Your next operation is to copy, using the COPY command, the formulas at the top of the Total Cases, Total Cost and Reorder Time columns, down the columns.

Leave your cursor on any location and type:

/C	selects COPY command and displays Range to copy from
G4	first coordinate to copy from
.	ellipsis—indicates from-to
I4	last coordinate to copy from
RETURN	displays Range to copy to
G5	first coordinate to copy to
.	ellipsis—indicates from-to
G11	last coordinate to copy to
RETURN	executes the command

Formula four, at the bottom of the Total Cost column, totals the cost of the entire inventory, and displays that amount in dollars and cents.

Place your cursor on H13 and type:

@SUM(	adds values in the list
H3	first coordinate in the list
.	ellipsis—indicates from-to
H12	last coordinate in the list
)	closes the list
RETURN	enters the formula

To format in dollars and cents, leave your cursor on H13 and type:

/R   starts RANGE command

F   selects Format option

C   selects Currency option and displays
                        # of decimal places: 2

RETURN   displays Range to format H13..H13

RETURN   executes the command

MAKING WORKSHEET ENTRIES

You are now ready to make entries to your DAILY INVENTORY REPORT WORKSHEET as illustrated in Figure 3.

	A	B	C	D	E	F	G	H	I
1	Item	Reorder	Cost	Cases	Cases	Cases	Total	Total	Reorder
2	Number	Quantity	Per Case	Rec'd	Sold	On Hand	Cases	Cost	Time
3	---	---	---	---	---	---	---	---	---
4	400	10	3.35	20	5		15	$50.25	NA
5	100	15	6.35	20	2		18	$114.30	NA
6	700	25	9.55	30	5		25	$238.75	NA
7	200	10	12.55	12	8		4	$50.20	1
8	500	20	8.75	10	1		9	$78.75	1
9	800	30	21.25	30	9		21	$446.25	1
10	600	5	3.15	3	1		2	$6.30	1
11	300	35	12.75	5	4		1	$12.75	1
12	---	---	---	---	---	---	---	---	---
13								$997.55	

Figure 3

Now you have entered your data and entered your Item Numbers. If your Item Numbers are out of sequence, you may wish to have all the Item Numbers in ascending order.

1-2-3 allows you to do this easily and quickly with the DATA Sort command. To accomplish this,

Place your cursor on A4 and type:

/D	starts DATA command
S	selects Sort option
D	selects Data-Range and displays A4
.	ellipsis—indicates from-to

Move your cursor to I11, with the arrow keys. The screen will reverse to display the area being sorted.

RETURN	displays options
P	selects Primary-Key and displays A4
RETURN	displays Sort order (A or D)
A	selects Ascending order
RETURN	displays options
G	selects Go option and executes the command

Your worksheet should now look like Figure 4.

	A	B	C	D	E	F	G	H	I
1	Item	Reorder	Cost	Cases	Cases	Cases	Total	Total	Reorder
2	Number	Quantity	Per Case	Rec'd	Sold	On Hand	Cases	Cost	Time
3	-------	-------	-------	-------	-------	-------	-------	-------	-------
4	100	15	6.35	20	2		18	$114.30	NA
5	200	10	12.55	12	8		4	$50.20	1
6	300	35	12.75	5	4		1	$12.75	1
7	400	10	3.35	20	5		15	$50.25	NA
8	500	20	8.75	10	1		9	$78.75	1
9	600	5	3.15	3	1		2	$6.30	1
10	700	25	9.55	30	5		25	$238.75	NA
11	800	30	21.25	30	9		21	$446.25	1
12	-------	-------	-------	-------	-------	-------	-------	-------	-------
13								$997.55	

Figure 4

Now that you have made the worksheet entries as illustrated above, and the worksheet is complete for the day, you may wish to save the entire worksheet for later use, or print it for distribution.

To save the entire worksheet, type:

/F	starts FILE command
S	saves
INVRPT	name of file; do not type spaces between words
RETURN	executes the command

Now that the formulas are entered, we will want to name certain columns to be used later for updating purposes. We will first name the Total Cases column as: TOTCASES. To do this,

Place your cursor on G4 and type:

/R	starts RANGE command
N	selects Name option
C	selects Create option
TOTCASES	name
RETURN	displays Enter Range: G4..G4

Move your cursor to G11 with the arrow keys. The screen will reverse to show you which coordinate locations are being named.

RETURN	executes the command

Next we will name the Cases Rec'd and Cases Sold columns as: RECDSOLD. To do this,

Place your cursor on D4 and type:

/R	starts RANGE command
N	selects Name option
C	selects Create option
RECDSOLD	name
RETURN	displays Enter Range D4..D4

Move your cursor to E11 with the arrow keys. The screen will reverse to show you which coordinates are being named.

RETURN   executes the command

Now we will have to save the totals in the Total Cases columns of the current Daily Inventory Report, so that they can be reentered in the Cases On Hand column before entering the next day's inventory information, to allow the accumulation of accurate totals in the Total Cases column of the new Daily Inventory Report. To do this type:

/F   starts FILE command

X   selects Xtract option

V   selects Value option which
                                      saves only the values

TOTCASES   filename

RETURN   displays Range

TOTCASES   name of columns

RETURN   executes the command

DAILY UPDATING

You will now want to update the worksheet to prepare for tomorrow's entries by entering the Total Cases file into the Cases On Hand column, as illustrated in Figure 5.

	A	B	C	D	E	F	G	H	I
1	Item	Reorder	Cost	Cases	Cases	Cases	Total	Total	Reorder
2	Number	Quantity	Per Case	Rec'd	Sold	On Hand	Cases	Cost	Time
3	---	---	---	---	---	---	---	---	---
4	100	15	6.35			18	18	$114.30	NA
5	200	10	12.55			4	4	$50.20	1
6	300	35	12.75			1	1	$12.75	1
7	400	10	3.35			15	15	$50.25	NA
8	500	20	8.75			9	9	$78.75	1
9	600	5	3.15			2	2	$6.30	1
10	700	25	9.55			25	25	$238.75	NA
11	800	30	21.25			21	21	$446.25	1
12	---	---	---	---	---	---	---	---	---
13								$997.55	

Figure 5

Place your cursor on F4 and type:

/F	starts FILE command
C	selects Combine option
C	selects Copy option
E	selects Entire File option
TOTCASES	filename
RETURN	executes the command

It will be necessary to erase the entries in the Cases Rec'd and Cases Sold columns to allow for tomorrow's entries into those columns.

/R	starts RANGE command
E	selects Erase option
RECDSOLD	name of coordinates
RETURN	executes the command

Your Daily Inventory Report worksheet is now updated and ready to have new entries made as you repeat the entry and updating process for the new day.

UPDATING WITH KEYBOARD MACROS

1-2-3 has an extremely powerful feature which is called Keyboard Macros, which allows you to set up a string of keystroke information in a small file, enabling you to perform an operation, such as the Daily Updating updating we just did, with a single keystroke.

To set up the Keyboard Macros, you will first need to enter the keystroke information into a coordinate or a group of adjacent coordinates in a column.

Next you will need to name the coordinate or group of coordinates which contain the keystroke information, using a backslash followed by any single character from A to Z. Example: \A.

First we will enter the Keyboard Macros file.

—————————————————— **NOTE** ——————————————————

An apostrophe (') is entered at the beginning of each line to prepare coordinates for label information.

The ˜ represents a RETURN.

We have put an r after the filename RETURN because the computer asks if you want to Replace or Cancel a file which already exists on the disk. The R represents the Replace.

{goto} moves cursor to the coordinate following it.

First we will enter the Keyboard Macros file. Place your cursor on A17 and type:

```
, /fxvTOTCASES˜TOTCASES˜r
, {goto}F4˜
, /fcceTOTCASES˜
, /reRECDSOLD˜
```

Second operation will be to name the coordinates containing the Keyboard Macros.

Place your cursor on A17 and type:

/R	starts RANGE command
N	selects Name option
C	selects Create option
A	name of coordinate
RETURN	displays Range: A17..A17

Move your cursor to A20 with the arrow keys. Screen will reverse to display coordinates being named.

| RETURN | executes the command |

Now that the keyboard macros file is named, to demonstrate its use, first make new entries, as illustrated in Figure 6. Your worksheet should then look like Figure 6.

	A	B	C	D	E	F	G	H	I
1	Item	Reorder	Cost	Cases	Cases	Cases	Total	Total	Reorder
2	Number	Quantity	Per Case	Rec'd	Sold	On Hand	Cases	Cost	Time
3	------	-------	--------	-----	-----	-------	-----	------	-------
4	100	15	6.35		5	18	13	$82.55	1
5	200	10	12.55	10		4	14	$175.70	NA
6	300	35	12.75	30		1	31	$395.25	1
7	400	10	3.35		10	15	5	$16.75	1
8	500	20	8.75	20		9	29	$253.75	NA
9	600	5	3.15	25		2	27	$85.05	NA
10	700	25	9.55		15	25	10	$95.50	1
11	800	30	21.25		12	21	9	$191.25	1
12	------	-------	--------	-----	-----	-------	-----	------	-------
13								$1,295.80	
14									
15									
16									
17	/fxvTOTCASES~TOTCASES~r								
18	{goto}F4~								
19	/fcceTOTCASES~								
20	/reRECDSOLD~								

Figure 6

To execute the macros,

Hold the Alt key down and press A.

Sit back and watch what happens.

Your worksheet should look like Figure 7.

	A	B	C	D	E	F	G	H	I
1	Item	Reorder	Cost	Cases	Cases	Cases	Total	Total	Reorder
2	Number	Quantity	Per Case	Rec'd	Sold	On Hand	Cases	Cost	Time
3	----	----	----	----	----	----	----	----	----
4	100	15	6.35			13	13	$82.55	1
5	200	10	12.55			14	14	$175.70	NA
6	300	35	12.75			31	31	$395.25	1
7	400	10	3.35			5	5	$16.75	1
8	500	20	8.75			29	29	$253.75	NA
9	600	5	3.15			27	27	$85.05	NA
10	700	25	9.55			10	10	$95.50	1
11	800	30	21.25			9	9	$191.25	1
12	----	----	----	----	----	----	----	----	----
13								$1,295.80	
14									
15									
16									
17	/fxvTOTCASES^TOTCASES^r								
18	{goto}F4^								
19	/fcceTOTCASES^								
20	/reRECDSOLD^								

Figure 7

SAVING

You may wish to save your entire worksheet. To do this leave your cursor on any location and type:

/F   starts FILE command

S   selects SAVE option

Type in name of file. Do not leave spaces between words.

RETURN   executes the command

PRINTING

To print out all or a portion of your worksheet, use the following directions, which are given for the Epson printer (compressed font).

Place your cursor on A1 and type:

/P	starts PRINT command
P	displays options
O	selects Options option
S	selects Setup option and displays Enter Setup String
015	sets an Epson printer to compressed font
RETURN	accepts setup and displays options
M	selects Margin option
R	selects Right option
230	characters per line
RETURN	displays options
Q	selects Quit option and returns to main print menu
R	displays Range to print from
.	ellipsis—indicates from-to

Move cursor, with arrow keys, to last coordinate in area you wish to print. The screen will reverse to indicate the area being printed.

RETURN	executes the command
G	selects Go option and prints

To exit out of PRINT command, type:

Q	selects Quit option and exits out of PRINT command

EXERCISE TEN

AMORTIZATION SCHEDULE

DESCRIPTION

The Lotus 1-2-3 program has some extremely powerful functions which allow you to calculate an unknown payment or principal of a loan.

To demonstrate this, an amortization schedule has been set up which first determines either the unknown payment or principal. A report is then generated which contains the term, principal, principal payment, interest payment, principal paid to date, and the interest paid to date for the length of the term.

OPERATIONS PERFORMED

Setting Up The Worksheet Format

Entering Mathematical Formulas

Making Worksheet Entries

FUNCTIONS USED

IF
MAX
PAYMENT
PRESENT VALUE
SUM

COMMANDS USED

COPY	copies formulas
FILE	saves worksheet
PRINT	prints worksheet
RANGE	formats in percentage
RANGE	formats in 2 decimal places
RANGE	centers labels
REPEAT	repeats dashed lines
WORKSHEET	adjusts column width

SETTING UP THE WORKSHEET FORMAT

To set up your Amortization Schedule worksheet, use the following directions, copy Figure 1 exactly as it is illustrated, retaining exact row and column locations of all information.

Enter your column headings.

After entering your column headings, you will center them in the columns by using the Center option.

Place your cursor on A11 and type:

/R	starts RANGE command
L	selects Label-Prefix option
C	selects Center option and displays Range of labels A11..A11

Move your cursor to F12. Notice the screen is reversing to show you which coordinates are to be centered.

RETURN	executes the command

To enter dashed lines on your worksheet, place your cursor on the left-most column of the row where you want the line to begin (A6 in this example.)

Type:

\	starts REPEAT command
—	label to be repeated
RETURN	executes the command

The column your cursor is on will now have a line of dashes across its width. To extend the dashed line in the same row across the remaining columns, leave your cursor where it is and type:

/C	starts COPY command and displays Range to copy from
RETURN	displays Range to copy to
B6	first coordinate to copy to
.	ellipsis—indicates from-to

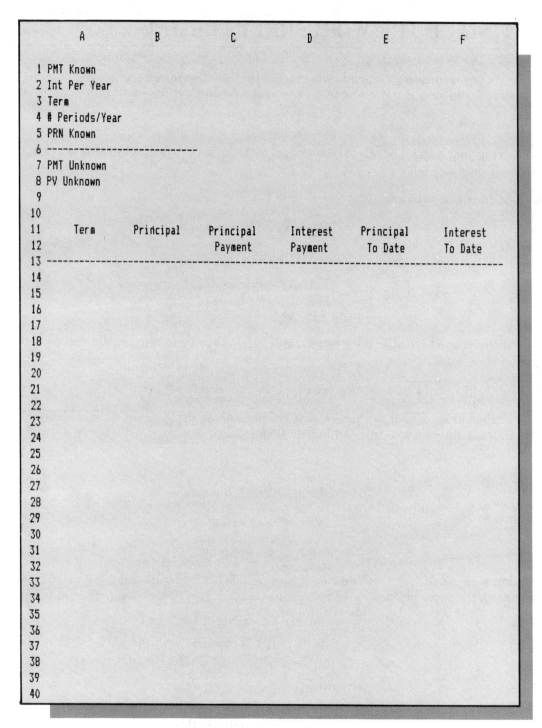

Figure 1

| B6 | last coordinate to copy to |
| RETURN | executes the command |

The dashed line will now appear extended across the columns you have indicated by your coordinates. To enter a double-dashed line on the worksheet, repeat the operations above, using the symbol = as your label to be repeated.

The 1-2-3 worksheet format contains columns nine spaces wide when it is first entered into the computer. Column width may be expanded using the following commands. In this exercise, you will use columns with 14 spaces.

To widen all your columns, type:

/W	starts WORKSHEET command
G	selects Global option
C	selects Column-Width option
14	number of spaces in columns
RETURN	executes the command

ENTERING MATHEMATICAL FORMULAS

You will now begin entering mathematical formulas that will establish the relationship between column and row locations. The formulas and their locations are illustrated in Figure 2.

Formula one, to the right of PMT Unknown, calculates the unknown payment.

Place your cursor on B7 and type:

@PMT(	starts Financial PAYMENT function
B5,	coordinate containing PRN Known
B2/B4,	Int Per Year divided by # Periods/Year
B3)	coordinate containing Term
RETURN	enters the formula

An ERR will be displayed until values are entered later in this exercise.

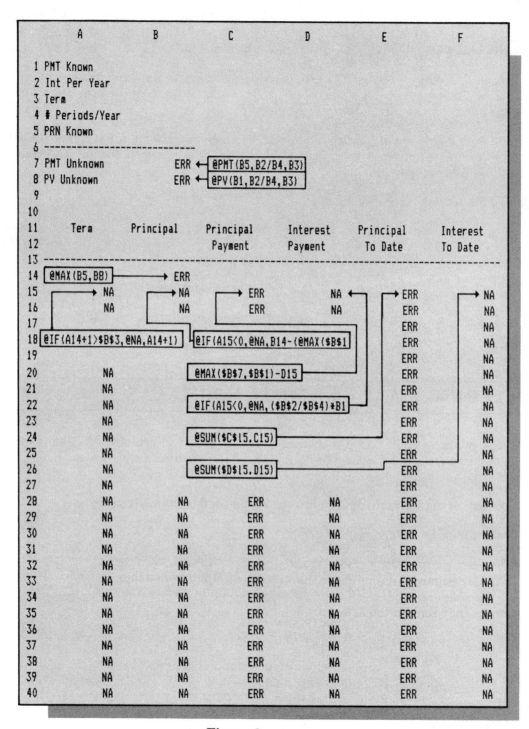

Figure 2

Formula two, to the right of PV Unknown, calculates the present value.

Place your cursor on B8 and type:

@PV(	starts Financial PRESENT VALUE function
B1,	coordinate containing PMT Known
B2/B4,	Int Per Year divided by # Periods/Year
B3)	coordinate containing Term
RETURN	enters the formula

An ERR will be displayed until values are entered later in this exercise.

Formula three, in the Principal column, immediately under the dashed line, determines whether to use PRN Known or PV Unknown as the principal for the loan.

Place your cursor on B14 and type:

@MAX(	selects maximum value in the list
B5,	coordinate containing PRN Known
B8)	coordinate containing PV Unknown
RETURN	enters the formula

An ERR will be displayed until values are entered later in this exercise.

Formula four, in the Terms column, determines the Term. When the term has expired, an NA will display.

_____ **NOTE** _____

1-2-3 is designed to do one of two things with coordinates when they are copied. The coordinates are either relative to their new location or they remain absolute, which means they remain the same.

A coordinate address is relative unless it is converted to an absolute by having a dollar sign ($) preceding the column designation and/or row designation, i.e. ($G$8).

A quick way to make a coordinate absolute is by placing your cursor on that coordinate and pressing the F4 key, which will place the dollar as shown automatically.

_____

Place your cursor on A15 and type:

@IF(	starts IF function
A14 + 1	adds 1 to previous term
>	greater than, logical operator to compare against
$B$3,	coordinate containing Term Note: $ converts coordinate to an absolute address
@NA,	selected if comparison is true
A14 + 1)	previous term plus 1, is selected if comparison is false
RETURN	enters the formula

An NA will be displayed until values are entered later in this exercise.

Formula five, in the Principal column, calculates the principal minus principal payment. When the term expires, an NA will appear.

─────────────── **NOTE** ───────────────

1-2-3 is designed to do one of two things with coordinates when they are copied. The coordinates are either relative to their new location or they remain absolute, which means they remain the same.

A coordinate address is relative unless it is converted to an absolute by having a dollar sign ($) preceding the column designation and/or row designation, i.e. ($G$8).

A quick way to make a coordinate absolute is by placing your cursor on that coordinate and pressing the F4 key, which will place the dollar as shown automatically.

─────────────────────────────────────

Place your cursor on B15 and type:

@IF(	starts IF function
A15	coordinate containing Term
<	less than, logical operator to compare against
0,	value to compare against
@NA,	selected if comparison is true

B14	previous principal
—	subtracts
(@MAX(	selects maximum value in the list
$B$1,	coordinate containing PMT Known Note: $ converts coordinate to an absolute address
$B$7)	coordinate containing PMT Unknown Note: $ converts coordinate to an absolute address
—	subtracts
D15))	coordinate containing Interest Payment Note: The value generated from this formula is selected if the comparison is false
RETURN	enters the formula

An NA will be displayed until values are entered later in this exercise.

Formula six, in the Principle Payment column, determines the payment made toward the principle.

NOTE

1-2-3 is designed to do one of two things with coordinates when they are copied. The coordinates are either relative to their new location or they remain absolute, which means they remain the same.

A coordinate address is relative unless it is converted to an absolute by having a dollar sign ($) preceding the column designation and/or row designation, i.e. ($G$8).

A quick way to make a coordinate absolute is by placing your cursor on that coordinate and pressing the F4 key, which will place the dollar as shown automatically.

Place your cursor on C15 and type:

@MAX(	selects maximum value in list
$B$7,	coordinate containing PMT Unknown Note: $ converts coordinate to an absolute address

$B$1)	coordinate containing PMT Known Note: $ converts coordinate to an absolute address
—	subtracts
D15	coordinate containing Interest Payment
RETURN	enters the formula

An ERR will be displayed until values are entered later in this exercise.

Formula seven, in the Interest Payment column, calculates the interest payment against the principal. When the terms expires, an NA will appear.

─────────────────────── **NOTE** ───────────────────────

1-2-3 is designed to do one of two things with coordinates when they are copied. The coordinates are either relative to their new location or they remain absolute, which means they remain the same.

A coordinate address is relative unless it is converted to an absolute by having a dollar sign ($) preceding the column designation and/or row designation, i.e. ($G$8).

A quick way to make a coordinate absolute is by placing your cursor on that coordinate and pressing the F4 key, which will place the dollar as shown automatically.

───

Place your cursor on D15 and type:

@IF(	starts IF function
A15	coordinate containing Term
<	less than, logical operator to compare against
0,	value to compare against
@NA,	selected if comparison is true Note: The value from the following formula is selected if the comparison is false.
($B$2/$B$4)	Int per Year divided by # Periods/Year Note: $ converts coordinate to an absolute address

*	multiplies
B14)	coordinate containing previous principal
RETURN	enters the formula

An NA will be displayed until values are entered later in this exercise.

Formula eight, in the Principal To Date column, determines the principal paid to date. When the term expires, an NA will appear.

_____ **NOTE** _____

1-2-3 is designed to do one of two things with coordinates when they are copied. The coordinates are either relative to their new location or they remain absolute, which means they remain the same.

A coordinate address is relative unless it is converted to an absolute by having a dollar sign ($) preceding the column designation and/or row designation, i.e. ($G$8).

A quick way to make a coordinate absolute is by placing your cursor on that coordinate and pressing the F4 key, which will place the dollar as shown automatically.

Place your cursor on E15 and type:

@SUM(	adds values in the list
$C$15	coordinate containing Principal Payment Note: $ converts coordinate to an absolute address
.	ellipsis—indicates from-to
C15)	coordinate containing Principal Payment
RETURN	enters the value

An ERR will be displayed until values are entered later in this exercise.

Formula nine, in the Interest to Date column, determines the interest paid to date. When the term expires, an NA will appear.

———————————— NOTE ————————————

1-2-3 is designed to do one of two things with coordinates when they are copied. The coordinates are either relative to their new location or they remain absolute, which means they remain the same.

A coordinate address is relative unless it is converted to an absolute by having a dollar sign ($) preceding the column designation and/or row designation, i.e. ($G$8).

A quick way to make a coordinate absolute is by placing your cursor on that coordinate and pressing the F4 key, which will place the dollar as shown automatically.

Place your cursor on F15 and type:

@SUM(	adds values in the list
$D$15	coordinate containing Interest Payment Note: $ converts coordinate to an absolute address
.	ellipsis—indicates from-to
D15)	coordinate containing Interest Payment
RETURN	enters the formula

An NA will be displayed until values are entered later in this exercise.

The next operation will be to format the formulas just entered, except for the one in the Term column, to display two decimal places.

To do this, place your cursor on B7 and type:

/R	starts RANGE command
F	selects Format option
F	selects Fixed option and displays number of decimal places: 2
RETURN	displays Range to format: B7..B7

Move your cursor to F15 with the arrow keys. The screen will reverse to indicate which coordinates are being formatted.

| RETURN | executes the command |

Next operation will be to copy all the formulas from Term to Interest to Date down their appropriate columns. For this exercise you will copy down to row 40, but you may copy it down as far as you would like for your own personal use.

Place your cursor on A15 and type:

/C	starts COPY command
	displays Range to copy from:
	A15..A15

Move your cursor to F15 with the arrow keys and the screen will reverse to show which coordinates are being copied.

| RETURN | displays Range to copy from: |
| | A15..F15 |

Move your cursor to A16 with the arrow keys,

| • | ellipsis—indicates from-to |

Move your cursor to A40 with the arrow keys and the screen will reverse to show which coordinates are being copied into.

| RETURN | executes the command |

As illustrated in Figure 3, enter your payment, if it is known, and interest per year as a percentage. Enter your term. Enter number of periods per year. Enter principal, if known.

To format the Int Per Year, in B2, to read as a percentage,

Place your cursor on B2 and type:

/R	starts RANGE command
F	selects Format option
P	selects Percent option
2	number of decimal places
RETURN	displays range to format: B2..B2
RETURN	executes the command

	A	B	C	D	E	F
1	PMT Known	151.47				
2	Int Per Year	12.00%				
3	Term	20				
4	# Periods/Year	12				
5	PRN Known	0				
6	-----------------------					
7	PMT Unknown	0.00				
8	PV Unknown	2733.36				
9						
10						
11	Term	Principal	Principal	Interest	Principal	Interest
12			Payment	Payment	To Date	To Date
13	-------					
14		2733.36				
15	1	2609.22	124.14	27.33	124.14	27.33
16	2	2483.85	125.38	26.09	249.51	53.43
17	3	2357.21	126.63	24.84	376.15	78.26
18	4	2229.32	127.90	23.57	504.04	101.84
19	5	2100.14	129.18	22.29	633.22	124.13
20	6	1969.67	130.47	21.00	763.69	145.13
21	7	1837.90	131.77	19.70	895.46	164.83
22	8	1704.81	133.09	18.38	1028.55	183.21
23	9	1570.38	134.42	17.05	1162.98	200.25
24	10	1434.62	135.77	15.70	1298.74	215.96
25	11	1297.49	137.12	14.35	1435.87	230.30
26	12	1159.00	138.50	12.97	1574.36	243.28
27	13	1019.12	139.88	11.59	1714.24	254.87
28	14	877.84	141.28	10.19	1855.52	265.06
29	15	735.15	142.69	8.78	1998.21	273.84
30	16	591.03	144.12	7.35	2142.33	281.19
31	17	445.47	145.56	5.91	2287.89	287.10
32	18	298.46	147.02	4.45	2434.90	291.56
33	19	149.97	148.49	2.98	2583.39	294.54
34	20	.00	149.97	1.50	2733.36	296.04
35	NA	NA	NA	NA	NA	NA
36	NA	NA	NA	NA	NA	NA
37	NA	NA	NA	NA	NA	NA
38	NA	NA	NA	NA	NA	NA
39	NA	NA	NA	NA	NA	NA
40	NA	NA	NA	NA	NA	NA

Figure 3

SAVING

You may wish to save your entire worksheet. To do this leave your cursor on any location and type:

/F   starts FILE command

S   selects SAVE option

Type in name of file. Do not leave spaces between words.

RETURN   executes the command

PRINTING

To print out all or a portion of your worksheet, use the following directions, which are given for the Epson printer (compressed font).

Place your cursor on A1 and type:

/P   starts PRINT command

P   displays options

O   selects Options option

S   selects Setup option and displays
                                Enter Setup String

\015   sets an Epson printer to
                                compressed font

RETURN   accepts setup and displays
                                options

M   selects Margin option

R   selects Right option

230   characters per line

RETURN   displays options

Q   selects Quit option and returns
                                to main print menu

R   displays Range to print from

.   ellipsis—indicates from-to

Move cursor, with arrow keys, to last coordinate in area you wish to print. The screen will reverse to indicate the area being printed.

RETURN   executes the command

G   selects Go option and prints

To exit out of PRINT command, type:

Q   selects Quit option and exits
                                out of PRINT command

INDEX OF FUNCTIONS AND COMMANDS

(continued on next page)

INDEX OF FUNCTIONS AND COMMANDS (continued)

Note: Some of the above functions and commands appear in more pages than listed in this index.